Desire, Market and Religion

Desire, Market and Religion

Jung Mo Sung

scm press

British Library Cataloguing in Publication data

A catalogue record for this book is available from the British Library

978 0 334 04141 2

First published in 2007 by SCM Press 13–17 Long Lane, London EC1A 9PN

www.scm-canterburypress.co.uk

SCM Press is a division of SCM-Canterbury Press Ltd

Typeset by Regent Typesetting, London Printed and bound in Great Britain by William Clowes Ltd, Beccles, Suffolk

Contents

Acknowledgements   vii

Series Editors' Preface   ix

Introduction to the Author, Jung Mo Sung   xi

Introduction   1

1 Theology and Economics: An Introductory Vision   6

2 Mimetic Desire, Social Exclusion and Christianity   30

3 The Contribution of Theology in the Struggle against
  Social Exclusion   51

4 Economics and Religion: Challenges for Christianity in
  the Twenty-first Century   76

5 Liberation Theology between the Desire for Abundance
  and the Reality of Scarcity   100

6 Liberation Christianity: A Failed Utopia?   129

Index of Names and Subjects   155

Acknowledgements

The reflections presented in this book would not be possible without the lessons, dialogues, suggestions, and critiques of many people whom I have encountered in the last 15 years. From among innumerable persons, I want especially to register my thanks to Hugo Assmann, Franz Hinkelammert, Júlio de Santa Ana, Enrique Dussel, Elza Tamez, Pablo Richard, German Gutiérrez, and Anne Stickel with whom I have had the privilege of discussing many of my ideas concerning the relation between theology and economics, whether in various sesminars promoted by the DEI (Ecumenical Department of Research), in San José, Costa Rica, or in more informal conversations. I also want to mention Ivone Gebara, Nelson Maldonado-Torres, Walter Mignolo, Alberto Moreira da Silva, Néstor Miguez, Lauri Wirth, Joerg Rieger, José Comblin, and Luciano Glavina who, in short conversations or in long working relationships, encourage me to seek continuously new perspectives.

I would like to acknowledge with thanks the translators of this work: Jovelino Ramos and Peter Jones for the Introduction; Jovelino Ramos for Chapters 1, 2, 3 and 4; Peter L. Jones for Chapter 5; and Archibald M. Woodruff for Chapter 6.

Series Editors' Preface

Liberation Theologies are the most important theological movement of our time. In the twentieth century their influence shook the Third and First Worlds, grass-root organizations and the affluent Western academy, as well as the lives of priests and laypeople persecuted and murdered for living out their understanding of the Christian message. In the twenty-first their insights and goals remain – unfortunately – as valid as ever.

Liberation Theologies are born from the struggles of the poor and the oppressed, struggles that were translated into an epistemological break with the whole of the Western theological tradition; that is, they are not one theological school among others in the canon. Instead, they sought and seek a new understanding of theology itself. The basis of that new understanding is the attempt to do theology from the perspective of the oppressed majority of humankind. Here lies the epistemological break: Liberation Theologians – whether Latin American, Black, Womanist, African, Feminist, Queer, etc. – realize that theology has traditionally been done from a standpoint of privilege. Western theology is the product of a minority of humankind living in a state of affluent exception and enjoying gender, sexual, and racial dominance. Oppression and poverty remain the norm for the majority of the world's population. By grounding themselves in the perspective of the oppressed, therefore, Liberation Theologies come as close as possible to being the first truly global theologies.

This series recovers the heart and soul of Liberation Theology by focusing on authors who ground their work in the perspective of the majority of the world's poor. This need not mean that the authors are solely located in the Third World; it is widely recognized that the First World/Third World distinction is today social as well as geographical. What matters is not the location of one's physical space but the perspective from which theology is done. *Reclaiming Liberation Theology* is the first to present the writings of a new generation of thinkers grounded in the liberationist tradition to the wider public. As such, this is the venue for the most radical, innovative, and important theological work produced today.

Liberation Theologies were born with the promise of being theologies that would not rest with talking about liberation and instead would actually further liberation. Let us hope that they will one day no longer be necessary.

Marcella Althaus-Reid
Ivan Petrella

Introduction to the Author, Jung Mo Sung

Jung Mo Sung is one of the most prolific and influential of a new generation of Latin American theologians, but his work remains largely ignored in the North Atlantic academy. Indeed, while he is author of 12 books, some of which have been translated into Korean, Spanish, and Italian, in addition to numerous articles translated into English, French, Italian, Spanish and German, *Desire, Market and Religion* is the first of his books to be published in English.

Sung, a Roman Catholic layperson, was born in South Korea in 1957, and has lived in Brazil since 1966. He is currently a professor in the graduate programme in religion at the Methodist University of São Paulo, Brazil, where he specializes on issues of theology, economics and education. He also works as a social activist, and acts as a consultant to social movements and base communities.

In his many books, Sung develops an agenda for Liberation Theology in a post-socialist and globalized world. Such an agenda is inherently interdisciplinary. Sung is clear that the most influential and dangerous theologies, those that affect the greatest number of people, are not found in churches or theological treatises, but in the social sciences, and most notably, economics. Marx once wrote that the critique of religion is the premise of all criticism. Sung would agree, but with a twist; the critique is of the religion found within the social sciences. They need to be the focus of the liberationist critique. For this reason, Sung's work reveals the hidden theology behind neoliberalism; that is, the hidden theology behind the reigning economic order. The social sciences, therefore, remain central to Sung's understanding of Liberation Theology, since they are ultimately where God's promise of life plays itself out.

If we were to situate Sung within the rich and wide panorama of Latin American theology, his work most closely bears the imprint of the Departamento Ecuménico de Investigaciones (DEI) of San José,

Costa Rica. I was fortunate enough to spend a summer in this unique and vibrant intellectual centre, a place where theologians, economists and social activists from around Latin American share research projects, meals and lodging. DEI has been a precursor of interdisciplinary work in theology; indeed, if it were located in the United States or Europe instead of in Costa Rica, DEI would be recognized as one of the world's most important theological centres. Similarly, if Sung wrote in English, German or French, his work would have the recognition it truly deserves. It is thus with great pleasure that this book is offered to you.

Ivan Petrella

Introduction

Desire, market and theology: what connects these three concepts? For quite a while we have had books and articles dealing with the relation between theology and economics that is texts that analyse theologically the dynamics of the market, and especially the way neoliberalism elevates the market to the condition of an idol. We have also come across books dealing with theology and sexuality, an idea that springs up in our minds when we talk about desire. Yet connecting desire, market economy and theology is not that common.

It is precisely for that not being very common that this book explicitly attempts to approach the logic that interlinks the three words. Rubem Alves has been one of the Christian theologians or thinkers most insistent on the role of desire in religion and politics. Perhaps the fact that he was one of the initiators of the Theology of Liberation, and that he studied and practised psychoanalysis, explain this emphasis. In one of his many fine books he states that

> if the mystery of religion is the mystery of desire, and if the mystery of desire is revealed as power, power is transformed into a new religion. . . . The place of desire is taken by the illusion of power i.e., the illusion that power can produce what the heart desires. The [Old Testament] prophets denounced this illusion and called it idolatry. An idol is an object made by human hands (praxis) to which power is ascribed to bring about the heart's desires.[1]

Nowadays the 'illusion of power' does not occur as much in the area of politics as in the area of the market. The neoliberal hegemony in the world has consolidated the market as the foundation and centre of our societies. The pursuit of wealth has become the most important objective for the lives of the majority of people, particularly those integrated in the market. Commodities have become *the* object of desire.

---

1 Rubem Alves, *O poeta, o guerreiro, o profeta*, Petrópolis, Vozes, 1992, p. 102.

I

Karl Marx, in the beginning of his book *Capital*, said that the wealth of societies where the capitalist mode of production predominates looks like 'an immense accumulation of commodities' and referred to commodity as 'an object outside us, a thing that by its properties satisfies human wants of some sort or another. The nature of such wants, whether, for instance, they spring from the stomach or from fancy, makes no difference'.[2] A want, which springs from fancy, has to do with desire and therefore the commodity has to deal with the satisfaction of both desires and, of course, needs.

If one of the functions of commodities is to satisfy a fancy, a desire, and if the satisfaction of the most fundamental desires of human beings has to do with religion, it is probable that there is a relation between desire, commodity and religion. Even if Marx's purpose was not to provide an answer to this question, some of his statements about the fetishism of commodity are quite stimulating for this reflection. For instance, he said that 'a commodity appears, at first sight, a very trivial thing, and easily understood. Its analysis shows that it is, in reality, a very complicated thing, abounding in metaphysical subtleties and theological niceties'.[3]

As a young man Marx had said that religion, a product of society, was the world's upside-down consciousness because the world was itself upside-down. He had explained religion from the perspective of the upside-down social relations. In his mature years, when referring to the fetish of commodity, he had, so to speak, a new encounter with religion. Presenting an analogy of the form of mystery in commodity he said that 'we must have recourse to the mist-enveloped regions of the religious world'.[4] It is as if he were closing the circle: to understand religion we must turn to the upside-down social relations; to understand the inversions in capitalism, and the fetish of commodity, we must (at the least it will help us a lot) turn our eyes to the world of religion.

This theory of the fetishism of commodity greatly influenced the Liberation Theologians dealing with the relationship between theology and economics. I believe there is a lot of wealth to be recovered and developed starting from this Marxian intuition of the relationship between economics and theology. Max Weber in his classic work *The Protestant Ethic and the Spirit of Capitalism*, where he sets forth the relationship between religion and the capitalist economy, also brings up

---

2 Karl Marx, *Capital. A Critique of Political Economy*, Part I, New York, The Modern Library, 1906, p. 41.

3 Marx, *Capital*, p. 81.

4 Marx, *Capital*, p. 83.

the issue of desire. To explain the reason why managers are, from the standpoint of personal happiness, irrational in subjecting their lives to a relentless work for their businesses, instead of subjecting their business to their lives, he says that 'of course, the desire for the power and recognition which the mere fact of wealth brings plays its part'.[5]

The accumulation of wealth, of commodities, as the only or the best way to satisfy the desire for power and consideration is acknowledged. This is one of the secrets of the dynamism of the capitalist system.

The introduction of the concept of desire in the theological critique of neoliberal capitalism sounds strange to many because the Theology of Liberation has been in dialogue mostly with social theories that have a structuralist and dialectical bent in their socio-economic analysis. For some, the utilization of this type of concept may well sound like a subjective 'shortcut' in the face of immensely grave situations such as the one of social exclusion we are going through. 'What can the discussion about desire contribute to the struggle against the social exclusion of so many people?' I believe this kind of reaction is understandable and fair. At the same time I also believe that our issue is a fundamental one.

Capitalism, as the readers of books about marketing and publicity well know, is an economic system centred on desire, not on the desire of profit by managers but fundamentally on the desire of consumers. Profit is a consequence of efficiency in satisfying the consumer's desire. It is because they know so well how to manipulate and satisfy the consumer's desires that capitalism and its defenders happen to get so much support.

If we want to understand a little better this fascination generated by the market system, and from there if we want to try to neutralize it in the best possible way, we will need to deal with the market–theology relation. And for this challenge I believe the following question is very important: does Christianity have any specific and relevant contribution to make to this debate? If Christianity and some of its historical formations, in line with their religious and humanistic tradition, have nothing important to say or do about this, ours is doomed to be another religion that survives by sheer social inertia.

Yet, beyond this apologetic concern, I do believe that Christian theology has inner accumulated wisdom useful and important for the unmasking of the perverse way in which the relation desire–market–religion is lived out today.

---

5 Max Weber, *The Protestant Ethic and the Spirit of Capitalism*, New York, Charles Scribner's Sons, 1958, p. 70.

With the intention of contributing to this work, I have written this book, which is divided in two parts. The first part is composed of four articles published in theological journals between 1994 and 1997, which deal directly with the relation between desire, market and religion in capitalist society. These texts were revised, enduring additions and rewrites, fruit of subsequent reflections, and edited to avoid too much repetition. Each chapter is autonomous in relation to the others, that is, they can be read out of order. At the same time, I believe that the four form a coherent and complementary set, analysing the subject from several perspectives. The original edition of the book, published in Brazil in 1998,[6] was composed only of these four chapters.

For this English edition a second part was added, with two articles that treat more specifically the question of desire, economics, and the struggle for the liberation of the poor in Latin American Liberation Theology. These two texts were written more recently, one in 2003 and the other in 2006.

The first chapter exposes in a systematic way the relation between theology and economics. The second and third chapters form the central nucleus of the first part and approach subjects like desire versus necessity, social exclusion and mimetic desire, and necessary sacrifices and idolatry. In these two chapters I try to articulate in a more systematic way the relationship between desire, market and theology. These texts written in different times complement each other.

In the fourth chapter, I analyse the challenges for Christianity born of the relation between economics and religion in the twenty-first century. For that, I briefly review the principal internal contradictions that capitalism was experiencing in the 1990s. Since the economy is changing rapidly these days, some economic data in this chapter is already obsolete; but I believe that the theological reflections are still valid.

The second part of the book analyses new challenges for Liberation Theology after the collapse of the socialist bloc and in the face of new economic and social realities and the evolutions, achievements and setbacks of communities and social movements. In the fifth chapter I analyse the tension between the reality of the scarcity of the resources and the desire for a society based on freedom and abundance. In the sixth chapter, a previously unpublished text, I analyse several positions within Liberation Theology facing the crisis of socialism and Liberation Christianity itself. From the experience of crisis of a nun who dedicated her whole life to the poorest, I propose a discussion on the source of Liberation Christianity's spiritual strength.

---

6 Jung Mo Sung, *Desejo, mercado e religião*, Petrópolis, Vozes, 1998.

4

Previously published by the author

'Contribuições da teologia na luta contra a exclusão social', *Revista Eclesiástica Brasileira*, vol. 57, n. 226 (June 1997), Petrópolis, pp. 288–313.

'Desejo mimético, exclusão social e cristianismo', *Perspectiva Teológica*, vol. 26, n. 70 (Sept.–Dec. 1994), Belo Horizonte, pp. 341–56.

'Economia, religião e idolatria: desafios para a Igreja no século XXI', *Convergência*, CRB, July 1997.

'Teologia da Libertação entre o desejo de abundância e a realidade da escassez', *Perspectiva Teológica*, Belo Horizonte: CES, vol. 35, n. 97 (Sept.–Dec. 2003), pp. 341–68.

'Teologia e nova ordem econômica', in José Oscar Beozzo (ed.), *Trabalho: crise e alternativas*, São Paulo, Paulus, 1995, pp. 49–72.

Theology and Economics:
An Introductory Vision

The good news and the poor

The joys and the hopes, the sorrows and the anxieties of today's people, mainly the poor and all who suffer, are also the joys and hopes, the sorrows and anxieties of Christ's disciples.

These fine prophetic words open the important document of the Second Vatican Council, the Pastoral Constitution *Gaudium et Spes.* Inspired by the Holy Spirit and enlightened by these and quite a few other prophetic words, many Christians and many churches participated in the struggle for the lives of all human beings, especially the poorest.

In the encounter with the poor, in the experience of solidarity, in the feeling of another's pain, in the indignation about the injustices and in several forms of struggle in defence of the dignity of all human beings, many among us perceive a privileged place for a true Christian experience of God. As Pope John Paul II said: 'In Jesus Christ every move toward man, as entrusted once and for ever to the Church, in the variable context of times, is also at the same time a move toward the Father and his love.'[1] In other words, there is no other way to God but the one that leads to human beings with the problems, challenges and possibilities resulting from their personal and social contexts.

Today, 1.3 billion people in the world have a daily income of one dollar or less. In Latin America there are more than 110 million people in that situation. Between 1989 and 1993 100 million were added to that total. The number is increasing in all world regions except in south-west Asia and Pacific Asia. Among the poorest the ones who suffer the most are women and children. Indeed women are the majority in this category. About 70 per cent of people living in absolute poverty are women. This is called feminization of poverty.

---

1 *Dives in Misericordia,* §1.

Beside these figures related to income we must also remember that even today there are almost one billion illiterate people in the world (in a time when knowledge is the fundamental instrument of work), more than a billion people without access to potable water, and the life expectancy of one third of the population of the poorest countries, most of them in Sub-Saharan Africa, is under 40 years.

All this is taking place in a global economy of 25 trillion dollars activated by great technological advances. This shows that the persistence of absolute poverty is not merely a result of lack of economic wealth. Economic growth by itself does not combat poverty, especially if the logic governing that growth is income concentrating as well as socially and economically exclusive. Illustrating this point is the fact that even in the rich countries, also called industrialized, there are more than 100 million people below the poverty line and 37 million unemployed.[2]

According to the UN *Human Development* report of 1997, the eradication of absolute poverty in the world in the first decades of the twenty-first century is a moral imperative that is perfectly achievable. The cost will be smaller than what many people imagine, that is about 1 per cent of the global income and no more than 2 to 3 per cent of the rich countries' income. Such resources could come from cuts in military expenditures and the redirecting of the resulting savings to poverty reduction and investments aiming at economic growth to benefit the poor.

It must be clearly understood here that an economic model geared to generating a maximum of wealth to be concentrated (as usual) in fewer hands is very different from an economic model geared to the elimination of poverty. The former, as is the case now, emphasizes both technological innovation and management aiming at reducing the number and cost of labour, thus generating the serious problem of structural unemployment. It also emphasizes a globalization centred in the financial market as well as in the free flow of capital and commodities only, not workers.

On the other hand an economy geared to the elimination of poverty would emphasize job creation and better income distribution as central criteria for economic and political decisions, whether on a national or global level. That is why the UN report says that the challenge to mobilize resources for the eradication of poverty is, more to the point, a challenge to restructure priorities.

In the face of such a complex and contradictory world, a world of

---

2 These figures were taken from the UN *Human Development Report*, 1997, available in the Internet: www.unpd.org.

so much wealth and misery, our gospel message cannot be abstract and generic. It must be concretely articulated in relation to the real historical context and to a new international economic order. In other words, it needs to be an announcement of good news to the poor and excluded, capable of unveiling the sin that moves the world and of revealing the action of the Spirit among us; an announcement which, anchored in our practices, is capable of sowing faith and hope in the God of life who in Jesus Christ was revealed to all the victims in the world.

A sense of urgency regarding the social problems aggravated in the last 15 years, plus the conviction that words and actions in solidarity with the poor are essential to our mission of announcing the good news to the world, led many communities and pastors to take an interest in the analysis of this state of affairs. After all, we cannot announce the good news 'in the variable context' of times, if we do not understand our context.

If it is true that the analysis of economic and political conjuncture is, fortunately, already familiar to our pastoral activities, the same cannot be said of reflection on the relation between theology and economics. Although this type of reflection has been around for more than 20 years in Latin America,[3] due to a series of difficulties many still ask: 'What do God and theology have to do with economics?'

Theology and economics

Theology, as we all know, is the systematic study (*logos*) of God (*Theos*). The main object of theology is not to prove that God exists, because this is a presupposition of theology; furthermore it is not possible to prove conclusively the existence of God. In this sense, God is more an object of hope and faith than of certainty. Without going into a great debate on this, we can say that the central object of theology is God, or, in other words, the discernment of the images of God.

St Thomas Aquinas said that we know more about what God is not than about what God is; and that, therefore, we cannot understand God 'in Godself'.[4] This means that we must not fall into the tempta-

---

3 Besides the books on Theology of Liberation, which have already dealt with the relation between theology and economics, we can say that the first book that explicitly assumed such relation as central subject was Franz Hinkelammert's *Las armas ideológicas de la muerte*, San José (Costa Rica), Educa-Dei, 1977 (translated into Portuguese by Ed. Paulinas).

4 St Thomas Aquinas. *Summa Theologica* (Q. 1, art. 9), New York, McGraw-Hill, 1963, pp. 33–7.

tion of thinking that we have a correct and precise knowledge of God, but rather we must acknowledge our limits and try to discern, based on the experiences of faith/revelation as narrated in the Bible as well as in the Christian tradition, the diverse images of God present in (and underlying) our lives, churches and societies.

Starting from this notion of theology, let us approach one of the first images of God as presented in the Bible, that is in the text about paradise and the creation of humankind. The book of Genesis tells us that Yahweh 'God formed man with the dust of the ground, and breathed into his nostrils the breath of life; and man became a living being' (Gen. 2.7). It is an attractive way of talking about God and the human being. God is introduced as the giver of life; because of that Christianity has always taught that life is the greatest gift we receive from God. God is the God of life; life is part of the 'essence' of God. The human being is introduced as a 'living being' (body + life), born out of God's hands.

In the biblical tradition there is not, or at least it is not dominant, the dualistic notion of the human being, which is so strong in Greek philosophy. In that philosophical and religious tradition the human being is a compound of body and soul, and the body is in a struggle against the soul. Salvation would consist in the salvation of the soul from the prison that is the body. That being the case, religion should care for the soul as it struggles against the material and bodily temptations. This leads to a radical separation between theology and economics.

In the Bible, contrariwise, God is introduced as the giver of life who is concerned about the life of the human being. That is why just after the creation of the 'living being' God 'planted a garden in Eden' with 'every tree that is pleasant to the sight and good for food' (Gen. 2.8–9) where the human being was placed 'to till it and keep it' (Gen. 2.15), that is, to cultivate the earth to produce fruits for the life of human beings. In the biblical tradition the fundamental contradiction is not the one of soul versus body but of life versus death. It is for that reason that Jesus says: 'I came that they may have life, and have it abundantly' (John 10.10b).

We all know that there is no life without eating, drinking, clothing, healthy housing, liberty and affection or acceptance. That is why the Gospel of Matthew (25.31–46) teaches us that this compound, which makes life possible, is the key point of our judgement before God. When Jesus set this point as the criterion he is not reducing salvation to a merely material question. Salvation does not come through concerns about eating and drinking, etc., for all, even the perverse, worry about these things for themselves and their families. Salvation comes through the pursuit of eating, drinking, clothing, housing, health, freedom, affection and acceptance for the little ones, for those excluded by society, those who cannot pay us back or reciprocate. Only those who are moved by the Spirit of God are capable of this kind of gratuitous action. Those who devote their lives to defending the life and dignity of the 'little ones' do have the experience with the God who is love; even if they are not aware of that.

The production, distribution and consumption of these material goods belong in the field of economics. Thus, in the biblical conception of God, there is no contradiction between theology and economics. On the contrary, whoever knows the God of life defends a life threatened by the forces of death and 'intrudes' in the economy, in the name of faith, to ensure that it be at the service of all human beings.

Economics and theology

Many think that the relation between theology and economics is a one-way street that goes only from theology to economics and that there are no theological questions in economics. In other words, this relation would be something that only theologians can see, in their attempt to justify the churches' 'intrusion' in alien territory, that is the economy. They believe that economics is a modern science unrelated to ethics and (even more so) to theology, which should deal only with 'heavenly' concerns.

What this group does not manage to see is that the economic science is grounded, as all sciences, on certain philosophical assumptions, and even more so, on theological and metaphysical assumptions. That is because economics deals with questions related to human and social life. The reduction of religions to private and 'heavenly' concerns, as was the case in modern societies, does not bring to an end humanity's great questions that religion dealt with in pre-modern societies. Some of those questions belong in the field of economics.

We can say that economic science has several levels, the most visible and well-known of which is the level concerned with the functioning of the economy. Usually this level is identified with the whole economic science. But this science implicitly also possesses a philosophy, and therefore an ethic.[5] Furthermore, there are also theological

---

5 On the subject see, for instance, Joan Robinson, *Economic Philosophy*, Chicago, Aldine Publishing Company, 1962; and Manfredo A. Oliveira, *Ética Economica*, S. Paulo, Ática, 1996.

assumptions. That is because all sciences and theories must be built on premises which cannot be proved and which in most cases are parts of a myth.

On this subject, Celso Furtado says that

> myths have waged an undeniable influence on the minds of men who strive to understand the social reality. . . . Social scientists have always looked for the support in some postulates rooted in a system of values that they seldom manage to explain. A myth entails a set of hypotheses that cannot be tested. . . . The main function of a myth is to guide, in an intuitive level, the construction of what Schumpeter called a vision of the social process without which the analytical work would not make sense.[6]

That is why Joan Robinson, referring to the problem of morality in the economy and in society, says that

> the moral problem is a conflict that can never be settled. Social life will always present mankind with a choice of evils. No metaphysical solution that can ever be formulated will seem satisfactory for long. The solutions offered by economists were not less delusory than those of the theologians that they replaced.[7]

Cristovam Buarque, on his turn, said that economics 'formulated a theoretical landmark which is closer to a theology of the productive process. As in the case of any theology, the economy was built on the dogmas that form its basic premises.'[8] And another important economist, J. K. Galbraith, who refers to the liberal ideology as the 'theology of *laissez-faire*', says that the defence of today's neoliberalism is based on 'deeper theological grounds. As you must have faith in God, you must have faith in the system; to some extent the two are identical.'[9]

If what the economists say is true, we need to unmask the theology implicit in the current international economic order that is being deployed as a result of globalization, the collapse of the socialist bloc as well as the technological and managerial revolutions. We must strive

---

6 Celso Furtado, O *mito do desenvolvimento econômico*, Rio de Janeiro, Paz e Terra, 1974, p. 15.

7 Joan Robinson, *Economic Philosophy*, Chicago, Aldine Publishing Co. 1962, p. 146.

8 Cristovam Buarque, *A desordem do progresso*, S. Paulo, Paz e Terra, 1991, p. 86.

9 John Kenneth Galbraith, *The Culture of Contentment*, New York, Boston, Houghton Mifflin, 1992, p. 82.

to show the nakedness of the theology that moves this economic order, which, due to its religious basis, fascinates people.

The importance of revealing such implicit theology or, as Hugo Assmann calls it, an 'endogenous theology' of the market system, will be clearer if we take two things into account. First, he who practises evil in the name of some perverse god (an idol) or, guided by a religious kind of devotion, has a peaceful conscience (see Psalm 73.12). This is so because the evil that one practises against 'the little ones' is not seen as evil, but as saving work. That being the case evil knows no limits. Second, to the extent that the capitalist system produces an 'economic religion', it manages to fascinate people both with its promises and its demands for sacrifice. A people fascinated by the capitalist 'religious aroma' struggle to enter the market's 'sanctuary', but not to build a more fraternal, just and humane society.

The theology of the new economic order

I will not deal here with details and dynamics of the new economic order, which is now being implanted in the world, but with its theological assumptions. If it is true that current capitalism has an endogenous theology, it must share some fundamental characteristics with all religions. For instance, the promise of paradise; the notion of original sin or explanation of the fundamental cause of suffering and evil in the world; and the way, as well as the price, to pay (the necessary sacrifices) for reaching paradise. Obviously these themes are not treated with a traditional religious language by the defenders of the capitalist system, but terminological change does not necessarily mean that these questions are not being addressed in a mythical-religious way.

Paradise and technical progress

A first point which must be clear when we talk about 'the religiosity of capitalism' is the fact that modern societies did not break totally with a mythical-religious view of medieval societies. In the Middle Ages paradise, or utopia, was the object of an eschatological hope. It was localized at the end of history, and was the fruit of divine intervention. In modernity this utopia was relocated from after-death transcendence to the future, in the course of human history. Now the utopia is not seen any more as an after-death fruit of divine intervention, but as a fruit of technological progress. It is the so-called 'myth of progress'.

With this myth disappears the notion of limits for human actions, to be replaced by the rise of the idea that 'will is power'.[10]

With this transformation of the notion of utopia and human action, modernity is the carrier of a good news that competes with the traditional religious good news. Serge Latouche affirmed that the bourgeoisie 'achieved its power thanks to the myth of the abolition of death in its three forms (violent, miserable and natural).'[11] Western civilization with its judicial and political system would put an end to violent death; with economic growth to death by hunger, and with scientific advances to natural death.

This myth-promise of eradication of death led to the transformation of the notion of death itself. Today death is not seen as a natural part of our human condition, but as a defeat for medicine in the face of the diseases and other social infirmities. This is so much so that the localization and aesthetics of modern graveyards are very different from those of an earlier age. Maybe the specialized business of freezing terminal patients is the most typical example of this myth. There are in the United States businesses that charge more than $100,000 to freeze the whole body or more than $30,000 to freeze just the head. The logic is as follows: death is seen as a defeat of the medical sciences regarding the disease. Before the end of the 'game' one asks for 'time' – the patient is frozen – so as to allow the medical sciences to develop and discover a cure. Then the patient is defrosted and cured. When caught by another incurable disease the patient will be frozen once again until new discovery. Thus this goes on successively as well as the search for drugs for all diseases – including the ones to 'cure' aging.

It is in such a horizon of utopian hope of the mythical religious kind, that F. Fukuyama affirms that the 'good news has come'.[12] According to him it is definitely proved that with the collapse of the socialist bloc, the capitalist market system is the apex of the evolution of human history and we are about to enter the 'Promised Land'.[13] Not the end of historical happenings, but the end of its evolution. He says:

---

10 About this dislocation of utopia in modernity and its implications, see, for instance, J. Habermas, *The Philosophical Discourse of Modernity*, Cambridge MA, The MIT Press, 1987; G. Marramao, *Poder e secularização: as categorias do tempo*, São Paulo, Unesp, 1955; and Sung Mo, *Teologia e economia: repensando a TL e utopias*, 2nd edn, Petrópolis, Vozes, 1955, chs. 4 and 5.

11 Serge Latouce, *A ocidentalização do mundo*, Petrópolis, Vozes, 1994, p. 25.

12 F. Fukuyama, *The End of History and the Last Man*, New York, NY, The Free Press, 1992, p. xiii.

13 Fukuyama, *End of History*, p. xv.

The progressive conquest of nature made possible with the development of the scientific method in the sixteenth and seventeenth centuries has proceeded according to certain definite rules laid down not by man, but by nature and nature's laws. . . . Technology makes possible the *limitless accumulation of wealth,* and thus the *satisfaction of an ever-expanding set of human desires.*[14]

For Fukuyama the secret of paradise, the satisfaction of all human desires, lies in the limitless progress that makes possible the accumulation of wealth. Yet, he does not explain how the human being, who is finite, by working on nature, which is also finite, can arrive at *infinite* accumulation. And here is the secret of the myth: the passage from 'finite' to 'infinite' without rational or reasonable explanation. The problem is that without this passage the myth of progress cannot be realized nor can it be said that we are about to arrive at the promised land. That is why this is 'mythical-religious', because it assumes a faith in a supra-human being or in a supra-human law of history to enhance such a passage.

Fukuyama, like many other liberal and neoliberal thinkers, credits this magic capacity to technology; not any technology, but technology that was developed 'in accordance with certain defined rules [that were] laid down not by man, but by nature and nature's laws'. And what is this nature that is able to generate such a powerful science? It is the same nature that, according to Fukuyama, moved the evolution of history in the direction of the market system. Likewise Paul A. Samuelson, winner of the Nobel Prize in Economics, says that the capitalist market system 'merely evolved, and, as in the case of nature, is undergoing changes'.[15]

The market system, of competition of all against all, is presented as the one that makes possible the endless technical progress which will provide us the possibility of endless accumulation that will satisfy all our current and future desires. Capitalism is presented as the implementer of the promises that Christianity made for life after death. The change not only concerns time, that is, from the next life to a historical future, but also concerns the implementer of the promises, that is, from God to the capitalist system.

In the face of the social and economic problems that persist in spite of all programmes of social adjustment and economic liberalization, the neoliberal defenders of the current process of globalization of the

---

14 Fukuyama, *End of History,* p. xiv (italics ours).
15 P. A. Samuelson, *Introdução à economia,* 8th edn, Rio de Janeiro, Agir, vol. 1, p. 45.

economy agree that its problems do not spring from the market system itself but from its not being fully implemented. They have such a strong faith in the market that when faced with social problems created by the market, they propose more market to solve them. They believe that the problem will be solved when the market comes to be 'all in all'.

For such a great promise as 'the limitless accumulation of wealth' which will satisfy 'all desires', it is necessary to have an immense faith; the faith that Milton Friedman, Nobel Prizewinner in Economics, demands from the critics of capitalism: 'Underlying most arguments against the free market is a lack of faith in freedom itself'.[16]

Original sin

When the promise of paradise contradicts the reality full of social and economic problems, one must explain the cause of such suffering and evils. Besides showing the way – 'the full market' – one must explain the origin of the difficulties and social crisis.

As is the case with other ideologies or religions, neoliberalism also starts with a diagnosis of the fundamental cause of social problems, that is, the fundamental evil (or, in religious terms, sin) which lies at the origin of other evils. One of the biblical texts that deals with this theme is the myth of the disobedience of Adam and Eve: what Christian theology has called 'the original sin'. Original, not in the chronological sense of the term 'origin', but in the logical sense, that is, we are not referring to the first sin in the history of humankind, but to the sin which is at the bottom of all other sins.

Hayek, on the occasion of his receiving the Nobel Prize in Economics in 1974, delivered a lecture that reveals the theological, epistemological and anthropological basis of neoliberalism. The title, 'The Pretence of Knowledge',[17] which brings to mind the 'original sin' of Adam and Eve, signals the basic question he dealt with. In the course of the lecture he defended the thesis that the attempt to re-establish economic policies with the intention of overcoming social problems is at the root of economic crises and causes great harm to society. This so happens because such attempts pretend to know the unknowable mechanisms of the market, besides going against its laws. For him there is no way

---

16 M. Friedman, *Capitalism and Freedom*, Chicago, The University Press, 1962, p. 15.

17 Friedrich August Hayek, 'The Pretence of Knowledge', in Assar Lindbeck (ed.), *Nobel Lectures in Economic Sciences, 1969–1980*, Singapore, New Jersey, London, Hong Kong, World Scientific, 1992, pp. 179–88.

other than being humble regarding the market and allowing its free mechanisms to solve – unconsciously – our social problems. In this re-reading of the original sin, the pretension of knowing the market and directing it toward the solution of social problems is at the origin of all economic and social evils. In other words, the greatest sin is to fall into the 'temptation of doing good'.

By the way, this is the title of a novel by Peter Drucker, the 'guru of the gurus' of business management in the United States. In this novel Bishop O'Malley says:

> 'Blessed are the Meek', it says in the Beatitudes. But, you know, Tom [a priest, his secretary], I've never seen the meek make any contribution or achieve anything. The achievers are all people who think enough of themselves to make high demand on themselves, people who are highly ambitious. It's a theological riddle I've long ago given up on.[18]

After this theology so compatible with the logic of the market, the bishop recommends that his secretary be an aid to the president of the Catholic University, father Heinz Zimmerman, the protagonist of the novel, saying that 'his only failure is in having yielded to the temptation to do good and to behave like a Christian and as a priest, rather than a bureaucrat'.[19] A good priest, a good Christian, is the one who overcomes the temptation to do good and acts like a bureaucrat, that is, fulfils the market laws, which, as we have seen, are compared to the laws of nature.

What we can do is fulfil the market laws, that is, the laws that rule the survival of the stronger and the death of the weaker, and not fall in the temptation of doing good. This means that we should not pursue the good but only avoid evil. But what is evil? Evil is wanting to do good, thus wanting to direct, or intervene in, the market. Therefore the only good we can do is to struggle so that I and other people will not fall into the temptation of wanting to do good, and under that guise wanting to intervene in the free market. With this interpretation of original sin we have a complete inversion of the love commandment. To love is not to be in solidarity any more with those who suffer, but to defend one's self-interest in the market (competition in the market) and to avoid the temptation to do good.

---

18 Peter F. Drucker, *The Temptation to Do Good*, New York, Cambridge, Philadelphia, San Francisco, London, Mexico City, São Paulo, Sydney, Harper & Row Publishers, 1984, p. 47.
19 Drucker, *Temptation*, pp. 129–30.

Yet, fortunately many people continue having the temptation to do good, the temptation to be in solidarity because they are still open to the Spirit of Love, the Holy Spirit. Against this spirituality of solidarity, neoliberals advocate the ending of what they call 'paternalism' and the introduction of a new spirituality compatible with a neoliberal modernization. Roberto Campos explicitly says that 'modernization presumes a *cruel mystique* of the behaviour and the cult of efficiency'.[20] A 'mystique' to overcome temptation and to assume a new cult. 'Cruel' because this new cult means subordination of human life to profit numbers, that is, it presumes a lack of sensitivity or cynicism regarding the suffering of those less competent and less efficient, the poor.

In concrete terms, in the current conjuncture of globalization with the adjustments imposed by IMF and the World Bank, there is no alternative for the poor and debt-ridden countries but to pay it with interest and to proceed with the adjustments (unrestrained privatization, cuts in social expenditure, reduction of the role of government in the economy and in social questions plus the opening of the economy) demanded in the name of the 'laws of the market'. It does not matter if these payments and adjustments mean unemployment and death for millions of poor children and adults. For neoliberals there is no other way. To look for other ways would be the pretence of knowledge which would generate even more problems.

That is why the magazine *The Economist* says that 'the best that the rich countries can do to help the poor world is to persuade their governments to adopt correct policies',[21] that is, to adopt the measures of economic adjustment imposed by the IMF and the World Bank and the liberalization of the economy according to the current dynamic of the globalization of the economy.

Necessary sacrifices

When one believes and has faith that all desires can be satisfied with the limitless accumulation of wealth made possible by technical progress, one also believes that the social system that generates maximum technological progress is the true way to 'paradise', to 'abundant life'. To the extent that one believes that the capitalist market system is this unique way, without any alternative, all is justified and legitimized in the name of the market. The market system is seen as the 'way and the truth' which lead us to abundant life.

---

20 Roberto Campos, *Além do cotidiano*, Rio de Janeiro, Record, 2nd edn, 1985, p. 54.
21 *The Economist*, London, 18 March 1995, p. 16.

Yet, we know that the absolute ruling of the market's logic means cuts in social expenditure and exclusion of the 'incompetent' (the poor) and of those who are not necessary any more in the current process of accumulation of capital. Explaining the nature of the market, Samuelson says that commodities should go where there is a greater number of votes or dollars, and also that according to this only viable logic 'J. D. Rockefeller's dog can receive the milk that a poor child needs to prevent rickets'.[22] He recognizes that from the ethical perspective this is terrible, but not from the perspective of the market, the only mechanism able, according to him, to coordinate economic processes in modern societies.

The sufferings and deaths of the poor, to the extent that they are considered the other side of the coin of the 'redeeming progress', are interpreted as necessary sacrifices for this same progress. Misery and death are facts which, as is the case with all facts, are open to diverse interpretations. Some interpret them as murder, and some as necessary sacrifices.

Those who share the utopian hope in the market interpret the death of a million people as necessary sacrifices. For Fukuyama, for instance, 'the bombing of Dresden or Hiroshima that in earlier ages would have been called genocidal',[23] are not genocidal because thousands of people who died in both cities indeed died on behalf of the market system and liberal democracy.

Mário H. Simonsen also says that what one can look for is to minimize, but not end 'the necessary sacrifice to progress',[24] and that the 'transition from one phase of stagnation or semi-stagnation to one of accelerated growth usually demands sacrifice which naturally includes a certain increase in income concentration'.[25] This means that the sacrifices are always imposed on the poorer population, while the richer sectors benefit from the life sacrifice of the poor which results in the increasing of their wealth. All this in the name of market laws that promise to lead us to limitless accumulation.

When sufferings and deaths are interpreted as necessary sacrifices we enter a vicious circle. To the extent that these sacrifices do not result in what the priests of the market system promise, we come to the crisis of legitimacy of the sacrifices. For these sacrifices not to be seen as being in vain, and by the same token for the market priests not to turn

---

22 Samuelson, *Introdução*, p. 49.
23 Fukuyama, *End of History*, p. 6.
24 Mário Henrique Simonsen, *Brasil 2002*, 6th edn, Rio de Janeiro, APEC, 1976, p. 28.
25 Simonsen, *Brasil 2002*, p. 58.

out just as murderers of millions of people, it becomes necessary to reaffirm the faith in the market and the salvific value of the sacrifices. It is then said that the sacrifices still did not produce fruits because they were not enough. Thus more sacrifices are demanded so as to ensure that the previous ones were not in vain.

Besides this fidelity to the logic of necessary sacrifices we also have the practice of accusing the 'proud' – those who have no humility before the market and try to intervene in the market – as guilty for the non-fructification of the sacrifices. The combative labour unions, the ecclesial movements and basic communities as well as the political parties of the left, are usually fingered as guilty for being against the necessary sacrifices, thus delaying the arrival of paradise.

It is important to take into consideration that this sacrificial logic is deeply rooted in the social consciousness of the West, if not the whole world. In almost all religions we find a theology of sacrifice, or equivalent. 'Without sacrifices there is no salvation' is a familiar idea embodied in our Western Christian tradition.[26] This type of theology has the great advantage of giving a meaning to suffering for people who do not know how to overcome it; and it has the great disadvantage of serving as legitimizer of the process of oppression.

The perception of the outstanding presence of the sacrificial process at the bottom of the social consciousness helps us understand why most people in our societies do not rebel against the capitalist logic. Besides sharing the consumer dreams of the market system the majority of the population find the requirement of sacrifices normal and natural as the way either to paradise or to the expiation of sins (of incompetence, failure and being poor).

Market, globalization and the Kingdom of God

The theology of the market as described above was taken from neoliberal economists and neoliberal theoreticians. It is not an invention of theologians. In spite of the fact that there are indeed professional theologians, such as Michael Novak, head of the department of theology of the American Enterprise Institute, who write explicitly theological books and articles to defend the thesis that the capitalist market system is the incarnation of the Kingdom of God in history,[27] we prefer

---

26 On the question of sacrifice in the West, see the important book of F. Hinkelammert, *Sacrifícios humanos e sociedade ocidental: Lucifer e a Besta*, São Paulo, Paulus, 1995.

27 Michael Novak, *The Spirit of Democratic Capitalism*, New York, Simon & Schuster, 1982.

to analyse the utterances of only the non-theologian professionals to show that capitalism is grounded in a perverse mythic-religious logic.

It is the presence of this mythical-religious structure in capitalism, which Marx analysed from the standpoint of his concept of 'fetish', that makes it possible for a person like Michael Camdessus, the general director of the IMF to present lectures on a topic such as 'Market-Kingdom: the double belonging'.[28] In this lecture to the National Association of Christian Directors of Businesses in France, he said: 'Market–Kingdom, we know well that these two must get married.'[29] After saying that the 'King [God] identifies with the POOR' and that in the perspective of the Kingdom of God and final judgement 'my judge and my king is my brother who is hungry, who is thirsty, who is a stranger, who is naked, sick or in jail',[30] a central theme in Theology of Liberation, he says that today Jesus urges the business managers and those responsible for the globalization of the economy to fulfil the mission of providing relief from suffering to the poor brothers and to expand the God-given freedoms'.[31] Following the inversion that occurs in capitalism regarding the love commandment, as seen above, he says: 'We are the ones who received this Word [referring to the text of Luke 4.16–23] . . . We know that God is with us in the task of making brotherhood grow. We are the ones who administer the exchange and also the holders of sharing. How is this, concretely?'[32]

How do we pursue the maximization of profit in the competitive relations of the market (the defence of self-interest) and pursue, at the same time, sharing and solidarity? Would not that be impossible or contradictory? Not for the one who has 'faith in the market'.

Camdessus says:

> You are men of the market and business pursuing *efficiency for solidarity*. The Monetary Fund was created to put the *international solidarity at the service* of the countries in crisis struggling to make their economies *more efficient*. The pursuit of efficiency in and by the market, and you know as much as I do, how related are efficiency and solidarity . . . .[33]

---

28 *Documents Épiscopats: Bulletin du Secrétariat* de la Conférence des Évêques de France, no 12, July–August, 1992.
29 *Documents Épiscopats*, p. 3.
30 *Documents Épiscopats*, p. 4.
31 *Documents Épiscopats*, p. 5.
32 *Documents Épiscopats*, p. 5.
33 *Documents Épiscopats*, p. 1. The italics are ours.

Camdessus establishes one circle: efficiency for solidarity and solidarity at the service of efficacy. As we have seen, thus far for capitalists the solidarity with the poorer ones (the criteria of the final judgement) is efficiency in the production of goods. And since for them efficiency is possible only in and by the market, the market is the condition of solidarity. For this reason Camdessus says that the 'market is an international solidarity'.[34] The difference and opposition between competition (in the market) and solidarity disappears. To be in solidarity, to be concerned with the problems of others, now means the defence of one's own interests against the interest of others. That is so because only the defence of one's own interests in the market would generate efficiency, and therefore, solidarity.

This 'magic', which transforms selfishness into solidarity, would be performed by the 'invisible hand' of the market (Adam Smith). It is the supernatural entity we mentioned before, the supra-human being able to bring about the limitless accumulation, the satisfaction of all desires and the unity of humankind. In the biblical tradition this is called *idolatry*.

But, as Camdessus himself knows, economic adjustments and the liberalization of the economy according to the proposed models of the IMF, the World Bank and the World Trade Organization, produce unemployment and other social problems in the less competitive countries. That is why he concludes his sentence by stating: 'the market is an international bond of solidarity promised with much eloquence but which comes slowly and often in an inadequate way.'

However, his faith in the market makes him believe that the market 'writes right through crooked lines', and for that reason he believes that 'sometimes inadequate forms' in truth are not inadequate, but [simply] the strange ways of the market in the process of bringing about a world of unity and fraternity.

In another conference 'The Market and the Kingdom in the Face of the Globalization of the World Economy', Camdessus dealt with the other dream of Christianity, unity and universal brotherhood.[35] He said that the gospel in announcing the Kingdom speaks

not about a complacent brotherhood – I was about to say paternalistic – but of a brotherhood which one builds on competition, tensions, and differences. A brotherhood that in the universe of the

---

34 *Documents Épiscopats*, p. 3.
35 Presented at the occasion of the XIX World Conference of the UNIAPAC, in Monterrey, Mexico, on 29 October 1993.

economy, must be lived out in the market and in the globalization; in the market where it announces and invites to sharing.[36]

Brotherhood based on competition in the market! Behold an example of the inversion of the concept of Christian brotherhood.

Christian theology and economics

In the face of this idolatrous inversion of so many human and Christian values; in the face of an economic system that deifies a human institution, the market, and in its name demands sacrifices of human lives in exchange for the promise of limitless accumulation of wealth, what should the attitude of the Christians be? What is the contribution that the Christian faith can bring to the struggle against the 'empire'?

If all that we have seen so far regarding a deified system has any basis we should take into consideration the saying of Marx that 'the criticism of religion is the premise of all criticism'.[37] One can critique only what is not seen as sacred. This means that our critique of the capitalist system will have a multiplier effect in society only if we manage to take away its 'sacred religious aura' and show that such religiosity is nothing but a perversion, an idolatry.

The theme of idolatry is a central point with several Liberation Theologians who deal with the relation between theology, economics and society. But this is not a concept restricted to theology. Eric Fromm, for example, in his a socio-psychoanalytic analysis of capitalist society utilized this concept with great ease. Max Horkheimer is another critic of capitalism who used it: 'Whatever limited entity – and humankind is limited – that considers itself as the ultimate, the highest and the only one, it becomes an idol hungering for blood sacrifices, besides having the demonic capacity to change its identity and to give a distinct meaning to things.'[38] With this we want to say that Christian faith and theology do have a specific contribution to make to the theoretical and practical critique of capitalism.

---

36 'Market and Kingdom', p. 11.

37 K. Marx, 'Contribution to the Critique of Hegel's Philosophy of Right. Introduction', in Karl Marx and Friedrich Engels, *On Religion*, Moscow, Progress Publishers, 1972, p. 37.

38 Max Horkheimer, 'La añoranza de lo completamente otro', in H. Marcuse, K. Popper and M. Horkheimer, *A la búsqueda del sentido*, Salamanca, Sígueme, 1976, p. 68.

Faith in the resurrection of Jesus and the critique of idolatry

The defence of the thesis that there is no alternative to the capitalist system is mostly based on its 'victory' over the socialist system. This victory is presented as the proof of the veracity of the capitalist proposals and its justice. All the other notions of justice, such as social justice, which conflicts with the notion of capitalist justice based on private property and laws of the market, are considered equivocal and contrary to progress.

This identification of victory and power with truth and justice (and basically, with God) is not new in history. The Jewish historian Flavius Josephus, in his book *The Wars of the Jews*, told of the pronouncement that General Agrippa issued to persuade the Jews not to begin a war against the Roman Empire. His reasoning is based on well-known facts of his time:

> Taking into account that all who live under the heaven fear and honour the weapons of the Romans, do you want to go to war against them? . . . Who will you take as companions to the war? . . . For there is no other help but from God; but that the Romans also have, because without God's particular help it would have been impossible for so great an empire to prevail and prosper.[39]

In earlier centuries, men had a habit of duelling to resolve their personal quarrels. The logic is the same. God is on the side of the righteous one who speaks the truth. Therefore the one who speaks the truth is going to triumph in the duel even if his argument is the weaker. That was so because God does not abandon the righteous one in the duel and will give him the victory.

This is the logic used by capitalists who say that the market system is fair and that the rich deserve their wealth. Among the critics of the capitalist system there are those who also use the same logic, but with the sign reversed. They believe that the struggle on behalf of the poor is a fair struggle and that for this sole reason, it will overcome. For them it is not that important if there are or not objective conditions for political victory, for they believe that God or the 'law of history' is on their side because they are just and, therefore, cannot be defeated, even if this victory takes a little longer to arrive. This type of trust has led, and still leads, many militants and well-intentioned groups into serious

39 Flávio Josefo, *Las guerras de los Judios*, Tomo I, Barcelona, Clie, 1988, pp. 258–60. [English language edn: Flavius Josephus, *The Jewish Wars*, trans. E. Mary Smallwood, Harmondsworth, Penguin Books, 1984.]

strategic errors by overestimating their political and social strengths, besides reinforcing the logic that legitimizes the capitalist domination.

The Christian faith is not grounded in this conception of a God who is always on the side of the righteous winner. On the contrary, it is grounded in the confession that Jesus of Nazareth is risen. That is the centre of our faith. To confess that Jesus, defeated, condemned and killed by the Roman Empire and the Temple is risen is to believe in a God who is not partnering with the winner (the Empire and the Temple). This faith allows the distinction between victory and the power of truth and justice.

Jesus' disciples ordinarily were not arrested for teaching that there was life after death, but for 'announcing, in Jesus, the resurrection of the dead' (Acts 4.2). The great 'revolutionary news' does not consist in affirming the resurrection of the conquerors and powerful, but of someone politically and religiously defeated, who, in God's eyes was 'the Holy and the Righteous One' (Acts 3.14).

In discovering that Jesus the crucified is risen, we discover that the established social order and the power-holders are neither righteous nor represent God's will. This faith moves us to witness the resurrection of Jesus in the only possible way, that is in defending the life and human dignity of the poor and the little ones.

Luke tells us how the early communities witnessed the resurrection of Jesus:

> Now the whole group of those who believed where of one heart and soul, and no one claimed private ownership of any possessions, but everything they owned was held in common. With great power the apostles gave their testimony to the resurrection of the Lord Jesus, and great grace was upon them all.
>
> There was not a needy person among them, for as many as owned lands or houses sold them and brought the proceeds of what was sold. They laid it at the apostles' feet, and it was distributed to each as any had need. (Acts 4.32–35)

This text, which is so beautiful, has something strange about it. The central message is the witnessing of the resurrection of the Lord: but this message is wrapped in two similar paragraphs that do not speak of resurrection but of economic questions: the collection of goods and properties according to each one's possibilities, and of their distribution according to each one's needs, aiming at not having needs among them. Those paragraphs speak about the sharing that transformed the crowd into community. One could say that the two paragraphs that involve the resurrection were there by a mistake of Luke and that therefore the witnessing of the Lord's resurrection has nothing to do with economic questions. Others could say, with reason, that, on the contrary, it is in the relation with concrete goods that one witnesses the Lord's resurrection. For faith in the resurrection of Jesus reveals that salvation stands not for accumulation of wealth, but for the formation of human communities where all people are acknowledged, irrespective of wealth and other social characteristics.

Faith in the resurrection of Jesus is an 'epistemological revolution' – a revolution in the way of knowing – which allows us to discover the true image of God and the human being. In discovering the true face of God and the fundamental dignity of all human beings, we feel challenged by the 'clamours of the poor' and called to build a more humane and just society.

The Kingdom of God and sacrifices

To confess that Jesus is the Christ, the Messiah, has other fundamental implications for our discussion. After the socialist-bloc crisis, the defeat of the Sandinistas in Nicaragua and so few victories after so many years of popular struggles in Brazil, many do feel like the disciples at Emmaus: 'We had hoped . . .' These disciples had hoped 'that he was the one to redeem Israel' (Luke 24.21). How could his small group manage the task of expelling the Romans, purify the Temple and thus redeem Israel? Because he is the Messiah! But his death on the cross showed that they were wrong. Now they were returning to their houses to wait for the true Messiah to show up.

The Jews that were present at his death also had said: 'Let the Messiah, the King of Israel, come down from the cross now, so that we may see and believe' (Mark 15.32). Coming down from the cross was the minimum that the Messiah, the one sent by God, could do. After all, if Jesus were really to be the Messiah he would have to do more grandiose things than simply coming down from the cross. Since he neither came down nor implanted the Kingdom of God on Earth, the majority of the Jews did not believe in him; they believed that the Kingdom of God would be established in its plenitude with the coming of the true Messiah, not by his force, but by the force of God, who would be with him. A defeated Messiah is not a Messiah.

At bottom we return to a theology which states that the victorious person is so because God is with that person. If this theology is correct we must admit that all those victorious in history were so because God was with them. We must accept that the Europeans who decimated millions of indigenous people in Latin America – and others who with their powers killed so many – were victorious because God was by their side.

Yet we know that this is not true. We know, by the resurrection of Jesus, that victory is not proof of justice; which means that the righteous does not always win. Faith in the resurrection of Jesus demands a profound modification in our concept of Messiah. To differentiate Christianity from this type of messianism, José Comblin affirmed that 'Christianity is not messianism: it utilizes the theme of messianism to say another thing'.[40]

The confession that Jesus is the Messiah demands that our conception of Messiah be no longer the one that associates it with fantastic and supra-human victories which would protect us from the provisional character of human history. To confess that Jesus is the Christ is to perceive that he is the Messiah not because of his victories, but because of his total faithfulness to the mission he received from God of announcing the radical dignity of human beings and in the name of this truth, the mission of confronting death and the idolatrous forces of the empires.

In this perspective, to belong to the communities that follow Jesus is not to have the certainty of our economic, political or social victories, but to have the certainty that his Spirit will be always with us, giving us strength and inspiration for continuing to announce the good news to the poor and to the whole of humankind – that all human beings, independently of their wealth, race or gender, are infinitely loved by God and therefore possess a fundamental dignity and are worthy of a dignified life.

If we believe that God was with Jesus and for that reason raised him from the dead, confirming him as the Christ, we should also arrive at other conclusions that result from this faith. If not even the Jesus who was the Messiah succeeded in fully implanting the Kingdom of God in history, it is because the Kingdom of God does not fit fully in history. In human history we can only build and live out anticipatory presences of the Kingdom of God: social, economic, political, cultural and religious relations that are signs of the presence of the Kingdom of God among us, in spite of their ambiguities and provisional character.

To affirm that 'paradise', the Kingdom of God or the Kingdom of Freedom are not built in human history is to affirm that 'to wish is not to be able'. We human beings are capable of wishing for what is

---

40 José Comblin, *O provisório e o definitivo*, São Paulo, Herder, 1968, p. 80.

beyond our human capabilities. Yet, there is more to be said. Affirming that is to deny the legitimacy of any demand for the sacrifice of human lives, whether in the name of the market, state, party or church, for all the claims of necessary sacrifices are made in the name of a sacralized institution which presents itself as the only way to building paradise. Since paradise cannot fit human history, no human institution is the carrier of paradise. Therefore the claim of necessary sacrifices cannot be made. The critique of idolatry in the biblical tradition consists exactly in this. It is for this reason that Jesus affirmed so incisively: 'I desire mercy, not sacrifice' (Matt. 9.13).

The Kingdom of God, paradise, is not work of our hands and, even less the fruit of our sacrifices in obeying the laws of the market, but rather the fruit of God's grace and mercy. And the full manifestation of this grace of the Kingdom of God will come about in the last days, when God 'will wipe every tear from their eyes' (Rev. 21.4).

To affirm that the Kingdom of God does not fit history is not to marginalize it. The contrary is true. The Kingdom of God is the horizon that brings meaning to our lives and struggle against the systems of oppression and exclusion. But, as in the case of any horizon, it is always ahead of us, no matter how much we walk.[41]

In order to prevent any equivocation in the understanding of our non-sacrificial posture we need to clarify the difference between 'sacrifices' and the 'gift of oneself'. Sacrifices are external impositions in the name of a deified law that goes against the freedom of the victimized person. They are claimed in the name of a deity (or sacralized institution) in exchange for the promise of paradise or for a reward. The gift of oneself is the fruit of love and freedom. It is a movement which is born inside the person and goes in the direction of either the beloved one or the one who nurtures solidarity.

The difference between sacrifice and the gift of oneself may be further clarified if we take the example of a mother who cannot stand one night away from her terminally ill child, even if there is nothing she can do in contrast to the nurse who would like to go to sleep but stays there as well so as to receive her pay.

Whoever, for love, is freely in the struggle as a gift of oneself, never feels that it was not worthwhile or that it was a bitter experience because it did not lead to victory. For the main motivation for the struggle was not the promise of victory but rather solidarity and affirmation of human dignity. But for those who undertake anything as sacrifice

---

41 On the question of the tension between the unreachable utopia and the social institutions, see: F. Hinkelammert, *Crítica da razão utópica*, São Paulo, Paulinas, 1985; Jung Mo Sung, *Teologia e economia*, ch. 5.

and obligation the only compensation for the bitterness of the struggle and even life is victory or reward. Without victory, what remains is the sensation of frustration for sacrifices that were not worthwhile.

In the gift of oneself we experience the grace that dignifies us and we understand what it means to say that God is love. In the experience of sacrifice we only manage to experience obedience to the god (idol) of the law. And 'where the Spirit of the Lord is there is freedom' (2 Cor. 3.17), and not the obedience to the law (of the market).[42]

'You give them something to eat'

We live in a very difficult time. Social problems are on the rise, as is people's insensitivity. It seems that cynicism is the spirit of our time. Even many Christian communities are falling into the same temptation of the disciples at the occasion of the multiplication of the loaves. Facing a hungry multitude that 'were like sheep without a shepherd' (Mark 6.34), the disciples suggested to Jesus: 'send them away so that they may go into the surrounding country and villages and buy something for themselves to eat' (Mark 6.36).

But who are these almost five thousand people, without counting women and children? Probably most of them were unemployed or day-labourers who did not find work and, as such, could spend the day listening to the preaching of Jesus. If that is true as seems to be the case, for Jesus 'had compassion for them' (Mark 6.34), whose problem does the disciples' proposal solve? Probably the problem of a small number, who had some money to buy something to eat, and the problem of the disciples' feeling of impotence regarding the crowd's hunger, but not the problem of the majority. It is as if the disciples had said to Jesus: Lord, let them be hungry far away from our eyes, so that our hearts will not have this feeling of impotence.

Jesus responds: 'you give them something to eat' (Mark 6.37). The disciples, not finding a way out of the market's logic, answer that they did not have that kind of money to buy that amount of food. Jesus knew that they did not have that money, knowing well that he did not preach pleasing things to the rich and powerful so as to get their financial contributions. But he knew what mattered most: the same logic that sends the poor away (the market's logic) cannot solve their hunger. For that reason he looked for an alternative.

---

42 On the problem of Christian and neoliberal liberty, see: Elsa Tamez, 'Libertad neoliberal y libertad paulina', in José Duque (ed.), *Perfiles teologicos para un nuevo milenio*, San José (Costa Rica), Dei-Cetela, 1997, pp. 41–54.

We do not want to discuss here the alternative proposal of Jesus at the occasion of the multiplication of the loaves. Even if we could arrive at a conclusion about how this multiplication really happened, that would not help us. After all we live in a world which is very different from the one of Jesus' time. What we really need is to be on the alert not to fall into the temptation of repeating that 'what the eyes do not see, the heart does not feel' and close our eyes to the hunger and suffering of the poor.

Our faith in the God of life, in Jesus, who came so that all may have abundant life, and in the Holy Spirit, the Spirit of love and freedom, must be witnessed through our solidarity in the defence of the poor and the excluded.

Our hope in the God who raised Jesus from the dead must be the basis of our spirituality for us to be the seeds of hope in the midst of the people, that is, the hope and dream of a world in solidarity, a truly humane world which unmasks the smallness of the market's dream of limitless consumption and accumulation.

Moved by this faith and hope, let us follow the steps of Jesus and the mothers and fathers of our faith as we struggle with courage and creativity for the lives of all, particularly the lives of the 'little ones'. Our struggle must happen on several levels: in immediate action of solidarity and defence of life; in short- and long-term action aimed at building a new, more just and more humane socio-economic order. Our journey is not easy, but is gratifying, because in solidarity and in the sharing of bread we experience the presence of the risen Jesus who goes before us.

2

Mimetic Desire, Social Exclusion and Christianity

Desire versus need plus redistribution of income and wealth

I want to begin this chapter mentioning a very common problem in the daily life of those who struggle on behalf of the poor. In the face of so much poverty in contrast with the wealth of a minority, which is characterized today as a 'social apartheid', it is very common to hear the call for the redistribution of income. This is so especially in a country like Brazil, which has the second worst income distribution in the world.

This demand is one of the main characteristics of the social speeches of Christian churches, in particular the Roman Catholic Church. Cláudia Fuser, studying the economic thinking of the Brazilian bishops, says that one of the key points of the economic programme of the NCBB (National Conference of Brazilian Bishops) is the distribution of income and immediate consumer goods. 'As an attitude of faithfulness to tradition, the NCBB always appealed to the government and property owners to promote a more equitable sharing of the wealth.'[1] Also in the course of the Second Brazilian Social Week, sponsored by the Social Pastoral Sector of the NCBB, which during those months had the participation of ecclesial base communities as well as of several popular and social movements, the theme of sharing was strongly emphasized: 'We want a participatory society where all people feel themselves united, free, and equal before the law and in the sharing of goods, while achieving full citizenship.'[2]

This appeal is justified not only by the contrast between conspicuous wealth on the one hand and blatant poverty on the other, but also because the level of misery and poverty is so high, demanding solu-

---

1 Cláudia Fuser, *A economia dos bispos*, São Paulo, Bienal, 1987, p. 203.
2 Setor Pastoral Social – CNBB, *Brasil: alternativas e protagonistas. II Semana Social Brasileira*, Petrópolis, Vozes, 1994, p. 60.

tions so urgent that they cannot be postponed (as many economists ask) for the sake of economic growth. It goes without saying that economic growth in itself does not necessarily mean a better distribution of income. An economic model aimed at the accumulation of wealth is very different from an economic growth aimed at overcoming poverty. As Cristovam Buarque says:

> Economic theory in Brazil never aimed at the problem of poverty. It forgot that production to enlarge wealth is not the same one that reduces poverty . . . With theories imported from rich countries, in the Brazilian economic science the word hunger does not appear, but only wage and prices; the word need is replaced by the word demand;[3] the objective of the productive process is not to satisfy the basic needs, but to increase consumption; efficiency is not in improving nutrition, but in producing for export.[4]

Furthermore, those who have been excluded from the market will not benefit from the economic growth if it is based only on the logic of the market. Added to this is the fact that the solution of our grave social problems must also involve the distribution of a fundamental good in our economy, a good that cannot be increased by human production: land.

This talk of the redistribution of income and wealth, which is so common among the Christian churches and other social groups, presupposes a point which seems obvious: there are many people who have too much or much more than they need, while there are also many who do not have the minimum for a dignified life. The solution of this grave injustice will also involve redistribution or 'sharing'. But what is obvious to some is not obvious to others, and it appears that we are dealing with one such case. Consider how difficult it is to establish a dialogue on this subject of a better distribution and integration of the excluded in the economic and social life of the country.

In truth almost all are in agreement on the need to solve the grave social problems that ravage our countries. But the disagreement begins with the means to do so. The point is that almost all are also in agreement that they do not have enough and for this reason economic policies leading to a reduction in their income or wealth on behalf of the poor, especially the excluded from the market, are not acceptable.

---

3 Demand is desire made viable by purchasing power.
4 Cristovam Buarque, 'A pobreza da economia', *Rede: Boletim Informativo dos cristãos de classes médias*, n. 11 (Nov. 1993), Petrópolis, Encarte, p. 2.

A distinction between 'having too much' and 'not having' presupposes a boundary that separates both sides. This boundary would be, for the defenders of income redistribution and structural reforms in society, the necessity of a dignified life. This thinking is grounded in the concept of human *need*.

The problem lies in the fact that in capitalist societies there is a great confusion between the concepts of needs and *desire*. For example, P. Kotler, one of the most important names of the marketing world says: 'When a need is not satisfied, the person is unhappy. An unsatisfied person will do one of two things – look for an object that will satisfy the need or to reduce the need. People in industrial societies try to find or develop objects that will satisfy their *desires*. People in poor societies try to reduce their desires to what is available'.[5] Kotler simply goes from need to desire, and that is it.

Liberal and neoliberal economic theories are conceived in terms of the satisfaction of the consumers' desires. But these desires are presented also as needs, and with this comes the confusion. So much so that even an author such as Jacques Vervier, a priest and a doctor of economics, says that the economic resources are always limited while 'the needs present themselves in absolutely unlimited form'.[6] Actually needs are not the ones that are unlimited, but desires. Explicitly assuming this confusion, Father Vervier says that to prevent ambiguities he prefers to avoid the concept of need and to use only the concept of desire. By doing that he assumes the notion that is much in vogue in today's economic thinking, that of a human being without bodily needs, a being just reduced to desires.

As Franz Hinkelammert says, neoclassical and neoliberal economic thinking

> assumes that man does not have needs, but simply taste. From this standpoint man does not present the demand to satisfy his needs regarding nutrition, clothing, etc., but only tastes or preferences, which allow him to prefer steak rather than fish, cotton rather than synthetic fiber, etc.[7]

---

5 Philip Koetler and G. Armstrong, *Marketing: An Introduction*, Englewood Cliffs, NJ, Prentice Hall, 1987, p. 4.

6 Jacques Vervier, 'Escassez, felicidade e mercado: ensaio de diálogo fé-economia', *Revista Eclesiástica Brasileira*, vol. 51, fasc. 202 (June 1991), p. 268.

7 F. Hinkelammert, *Crítica da razão utópica*, São Paulo, Paulinas, 1986, p. 63.

It is significant that an author who is at the same time a priest and economist, and who intends to articulate the relation of Christian faith and economics, assumes this identification of desire and need. Such identification blots out the concept of human needs. Christianity, on the contrary, promotes the notion of human being based on the distinction between the concepts of need and desire. To that effect look at the famous text of Matt. 25.31–46 where Jesus sets the concern about the neighbour's basic needs (food, drink, house, health, etc.) as the criterion of salvation; or at the text of Acts 4.32–35 where the practical witness of the faith in the resurrection of Jesus consisted in that 'there was not a needy person among them'. The example of Father Vervier's text shows the great confusion that exists in our capitalist society, caused by the negation of the difference between desire and need.

When the needs and desires lose their specific differences, whether due to the difficulty of establishing them, or to a theoretical option, the dialogue about income and wealth redistribution becomes very difficult. Let's take a small example. Does a person who lives in a $250,000 house, has a $100,000 beach house, an imported $80,000 car and the equivalent of $500,000 in financial investments have too much or too little? It depends on the employed criterion. If it is the one of need, that person has more than what is needed and therefore has some to share, as well. But that person can argue that a lot is still needed to fulfil his/ her desire to live in a $1m house and to own an island plus a $400,000 imported car plus a private jet.

When one thinks from the standpoint of desires there are no limits. One pursues the limitless. And when one desires the limitless there is never anything left to share. There is never enough. Therefore one does not accept a dialogue on income and wealth redistribution.

To understand the differences between need and desire, their relationship, and the role of desire in the capitalist economy is fundamental in order to advance in our struggle for a fairer and more humane society.

Economic development and mimetic desire

If it is true that without income and wealth redistribution we will not be able to solve our social problems, it is also true that our speech cannot stay just at this level. Income distribution or its concentration is determined to a great extent by the production process.

The development model adopted in Latin America in the period between World War Two and the decade of the 1970s was the one of 'import substitution', based on the ideology of developmentism that Celso Furtado called 'the myth of development', according to which *'economic development,* as practised by the countries that led the industrial revolution can be universalized'.[8] More precisely, there was the pretension that the consumption pattern of the minority of the rich countries would be accessible to the great masses in Third World countries. It is important to remember that this consumption pattern was determined by the 'consumerist anxiety that capitalism managed to disseminate in the consciousness of humankind, a pattern identified with a schizophrenically accelerated pursuit as the justification not only of the economic activity but also of the civilizational process'.[9]

This idea, a prolongation of the myth of progress which guided modernity, generated in our countries a type of modernization characterized by the consumption innovations of local elites without the corresponding development in the productive sphere. This development model 'aggravated the prevailing income and wealth concentration, especially in the phase of substitutive industrialization', in view of the fact that 'the adoption of imitated patterns of consumption of societies with far superior level of wealth makes social dualism unavoidable'.[10]

With the external debt crisis of the early 1980s, which generated the 'lost decade' in economic and social terms, there was a change of the economic model – we went from developmentism to 'economic adjustment'. However, the modernization model, based in the imitation of the consumption patterns of rich countries, was maintained and the 'accommodation' of our economies to the demands of the international market was carried out. For Celso Furtado it is fundamental that we abandon the illusions of 'a modernity which condemns us to a sterilizing cultural mimicry' and that we escape 'the obsession of reproducing the profile of those who define themselves as developed' and also that we assume 'our own identity'[11] so as to overcome the economic and social dualism which characterizes Brazil. For him it is fundamental

---

8 Celso Furtado, O *mito do desenvolvimento econômico,* Rio de Janeiro, Paz e Terra, 1974, p. 16.

9 Cristovam Buarque, *A desordem do progresso: o fim da era dos economistas e a construção do futuro,* 2nd edn, Rio de Janeiro, Paz e Terra, 1990, p. 132.

10 Celso Furtado, *Brasil: a construção interrompida,* 2nd edn, Rio de Janeiro, Paz e Terra, 1992, p. 44. For an enlarged discussion of the development models adopted in Latin America and their relationship with theology, see: Jung Mo Sung, *Deus numa economia sem coração: neoliberalismo e probreza,* S. Paulo, Paulinas, 1992.

11 Furtado, *Brasil,* pp. 78–9.

that we create a new conception of development within the reach of all and capable of preserving the ecological balance.

In line with that, Plinio Sampaio says that cultural dependence, jointly with the unequal diffusion of the technology and financial dependence, make out the main characteristics of the *new dependence*. For him the transformations in the pattern of capitalist development intensified cultural dependence. 'The technological progress in the area of transport and communication exacerbated the cultural mimicry driving to an extreme the tendency of the middle and upper classes to copy the patterns of behaviour and consumption of their counterparts in the countries that control the world economy'.[12] As we saw above, growing income concentration and increasing social exclusion are the perverse effects of this form of infusion of technical progress in the peripheral societies. That is because due to the prevailing difference in the average labour productivity between the technologically advanced countries and ours, income concentration is the only way for the acculturated elites to obtain the needed average income in order to have access to the opulent levels of life of the central economies: the wider the gap between developed and underdeveloped, the greater the necessary social inequality.

In the centre of the analysis of social dualism, or social exclusion, by Celso Furtado and also by Sampaio, we find the problem of imitation, of *mimesis* in the economic dynamics. We assume as our model to be imitated those who call themselves developed and we alienate ourselves from our own reality and identity. This mimetic desire has guided our economy and generated a brutal income concentration as well as a social and economic dualism. As a result, we have not only a huge social inequality, with the exclusion of an important sector of the population from the economic and social benefits, but also a separation between two Brazils which communicate less and less through the processes of production owing to their very different levels of participation in the world-wide technological revolution. This is one of the reasons why some authors have used the term 'social apartheid'.

The problem lies in the fact that it is not easy to overcome this mimetic desire regarding consumption, or, in the words of René Girard, mimetic desire of appropriation.[13] This type of mimetic desire is at the real centre of the modernity in which we live. This modernity is characterized by the myth of progress and the construction of a

---

12 Plínio de Arruda Sampaio Jr., 'Dependência e Barbárie', *Teoria & Debate*, n. 34, March–May 1997, São Paulo, pp. 57–60. Quoted from p. 60.

13 René Girard, *Violence and the Sacred*, Baltimore and London, Johns Hopkins University Press, 1977.

new type of utopia. The religious utopia or the eschatological hope of the Middle Ages became secularized and transformed into a utopian opening of the horizon of expectation from the standpoint of the concept of progress.[14] 'Paradise' was removed from the hereafter to the future mediated by technological progress. With that, the notion of limits for human action disappeared.

It is this revolution in the conception of history and human possibilities that leads, for instance, Fukuyama to say that 'technology makes possible the limitless accumulation of wealth, and thus the satisfaction of an ever-expanding set of human desires'.[15] For those who think like him, the clue for the satisfaction of all desires, both the current and future ones, lies in technological progress made possible by the system of free market. What few have perceived is that the clue for this technological progress lies in mimetic desire.

Friedrich Hayek, the 'pope' of neoliberalism, is one of those who understood this. He says that one of the characteristics of modern societies is that the majority of things that individuals strive to achieve can be obtained only through technological advances. That is the dynamic of progress. The benefits of the new knowledge can be dispensed only gradually, 'and the ambition of the many will always be determined by what is as yet accessible only to the few'.[16]

It is because the majority – imitating the elite's desire for consumption – also desire to consume the novelties of progress that this same progress proceeds by increasing the production of these goods for the masses. Thus he says:

At first, a new good is commonly 'the caprice of the chosen few before it becomes a *public need* and forms part of the necessities of life. For the luxuries of today are the necessities of tomorrow.' Furthermore, the new things will often become available to the greater part of the people only *because* for some time they have been luxuries of the few.[17]

---

14 See, for example, J. Habermas, *Discurso da modernidade*, Lisbon, D. Quixote, 1990 [English language edn: Jürgen Habermas, *The Philosophical Discourse of Modernity: Twelve Lectures*, trans. Frederick G. Lawrence, Cambridge, Mass., MIT Press, 1990]; M. Horkheimer, *Origenes da filosofia burguesa da hostória*, Lisbon, Presença, nd; Jung Mo Sung, *Teologia e economia: repensando a TL e utopias*, Petrópolis, Vozes, 1994, ch. 4.

15 F. Fukuyama, *The End of History and the Last Man*, New York, N.Y., The Freedom Press, 1992, p. xiv. The italics are ours.

16 Friedrich A. Hayek, *The Constitution of Liberty*, Chicago, The University Press, 1960, p. 42.

17 Hayek, *Constitution*, p. 43. The first italic is ours.

He says that 'today's luxuries', meaning the objects of desire, 'are tomorrow's needs'. Here is a subtle passage from desire to need. We'll come back to this point later on.

As a consequence of this position Hayek defends the idea that economic production must be aimed at satisfying the desires of the elite because these will be the future needs of the masses. And for the massification of the production of these goods, progress is a must.

The need for progress, which generates this enlargement of production, results from the fact that 'most of what we strive for are things we want because others already have them'.[18] That being the case, for Hayek mimetic desire is the mover of progress. 'Yet a progressive society, while relying on this process of learning and imitation, recognizes the desires it creates only as a spur to further effort. It does not guarantee the results to everyone.'[19]

The incentive to mimetic desire on the part of capitalist societies is not an abstract and generic one. On the contrary, society only accepts the desires that the market creates as incitement to enter the market 'war'. The market is the criterion for desires, whether acceptable or not.

The lack of a guarantee of positive results, or, even more, the impossibility that all obtain positive results, logically proceeds from the structure of mimetic desire and from the dynamics of the modern economy. The basic structure of mimetic desire consists in the fact that I desire an object not for the object in itself but because another person desires it. Thus, desired by both, the object is always scarce in relation to the subjects of the desire. It is because it is scarce that it is the object of desire. That creates a rivalry between the two who desire the same object. This rivalry or conflict has the modern name of competition, what the liberal economists call the mover of progress. Rivalry and competition are concepts opposed to solidarity and community. Furthermore in the dynamics of the capitalist economy, always with novelties, which are objects of desire, scarcity (always in relation to desires) is a basic fact. Thus the resulting rivalry and violence are endemic. They are always occurring.

This means that there will always be unsatisfied people in the dynamics of the mimetic desire. Hayek acknowledges this and affirms that capitalist society 'disregards the pain of unfulfilled desire aroused by the example of others. It appears cruel because it increases the desire of all in proportion as it increases its gifts to some. Yet so long

18 Hayek, *Constitution*, p. 45.
19 Hayek, *Constitution*, p. 45.

as it remains a progressive society, some must lead, and the rest must follow.'[20]

In truth, the dissatisfaction touches everybody. Even those integrated in the market with high acquisitive power live in eternal dissatisfaction because the model of desire is always innovating in its consumption thus leading to a race for more consumption. In reality it is an endless race for limitless consumption trying to satisfy fully and definitely all desires. The problem is that it is impossible to fully satisfy all consumption desires, whether due to the scarcity of material goods, the limitation of natural resources and ecological limitations, or to the fact that the object is desired precisely because it is scarce and also because the object of desire is always changing. Of course, those dissatisfied people mentioned by Hayek are not these but those not sufficiently capable of having a high consumption pattern and those who through the process of competition were excluded from the market.

Some might ask: why remain in that dynamic of progress–desire–mimetic desire, if the inevitable result is the frustration of many, if not all? The answer given must be understood as part of modernity's myth of progress. Embracing the illusion that technological progress will take us to the earthly paradise, Hayek says:

> The aspirations of the great mass of the world's population can today be satisfied only by rapid material progress. There can be little doubt that in their present mood a serious disappointment of their expectations would lead to grave international friction – indeed, it would probably lead to war. The peace of the world and, with it, civilization itself thus depends on continued progress at a fast rate. At this juncture we are therefore not only the creatures but the captives of progress; even if we wished to, we could not lay back and enjoy at leisure what we have achieved. Our task must be to continue to lead, to move ahead along the pass which so many are trying to tread in our wake.[21]

Here we have a *mystical* speech in the literal sense of the word. The elite of world capitalism become the guiding prophets of humankind in the journey toward the Promised Land. It is a very hard task which they themselves would not like to carry out. However, as in the case of the true prophets, they feel themselves 'captive' of this mission. They have not the heart to turn themselves away from the suffering

---

20 Hayek, *Constitution*, p. 45.
21 Hayek, *Constitution*, pp. 52–3.

of the people and 'leisurely enjoy' what they have already achieved. It is as if a mysterious force from God were burning inside their chests, moving them forward in the mission of guiding the rest of the world by their example, toward progress, toward paradise. Obviously this unrestrained pursuit of new and more consumer goods threatens the ecological balance and, by the competition's own logic (of the 'survival of the strongest'), many – the 'weak' – will be excluded from the market, and sacrificed during the journey. Yet they will say that these are necessary sacrifices for the sake of progress.

In absolutizing the market, in assuming the market's logic as something omnipotent, capable of producing supra-human results, against which we should not show any resistance, neoliberals end up confessing themselves impotent in the face of the market. This omnipotence, which consists in being able to set the logic of capitalist accumulation and its rationality (restricted to the estimation of costs and benefits) above the rebuilding of human life, results in our impotence to come up with any resistance to it, the inability of not being able to try any move for a greater inclusion of people, for the survival of the excluded ones, and, above all, for the survival of the environment which alone makes human life viable. This is what Franz Hinkelammert called 'the impotence of omnipotence'.[22]

Celso Furtado proposes that we should pursue a conception of development without the mimetism that has generated dualism and social crisis. On the other hand Hayek defended the logic of mimetic desire as the central axis and mover of economic progress. Furtado wants to combat the social dualism, while for Hayek dualism is a logical need in the dynamics of progress. Furtado looks for the satisfaction of the basic needs of the whole population; Hayek looks for the satisfaction of desires transformed into needs, and therefore deletes or 'forgets' the basic needs. These two authors represent two opposite postures in the face of the bourgeois modernity we are living through.

However, independently from these two distinct interpretations of reality, one cannot deny an obvious fact: in Latin America, post-war economic development generated only a modest social development. What then explains the maintenance of the model of development based in mimesis? It is clear that the economic, political and military power of the elites is there for its maintenance, but how to explain the adherence, or at least the passivity, of the masses?

---

22 Franz Hinkelammert, 'Una sociedade en la que todos quepan: de la impotencia de la omnipotencia', in José Duque (ed.), *Por una sociedade donde todos quepan todos*, San Jose (Costa Rica), DEI, 1996, p. 379–91.

The promise of paradise and necessary sacrifices

I want to present here three hypotheses which can be complementary. The first is linked to the dynamism of economic growth. To the extent that the economy grows, as was the case up to the early 1980s, the promise that in the future, through this same economic growth, it will be possible to satisfy the needs and desires transformed into needs of the masses, becomes a plausible promise. The myths of progress and development always had in their favour the postponing of the promises (fulfilment). This is part of the logic of the myths. The only prerequisite is that there be visible signs of progress as a guarantee to the masses that their dreams will come true in the future. A famous sentence by Brasil's former Finance Minister, Delfin Neto, expresses this logic: 'One has to wait for the cake to grow before one divides it.'

The second hypothesis, which complements the first, is linked to a characteristic of modernity related to mimetic desires. In premodern societies mimetic desires were suppressed or controlled on account of the violence they might cause in human communities.[23] Taboos, myths and rituals were institutional mechanisms aimed at protecting the community against internal violence, which in extreme cases could lead to its dissolution. According to Girard 'in archaic societies, prohibitions are closely interlocked and the different compartments they establish determine the distribution of disposable objects between the members of the culture'.[24] It is clear that, to the extent that the desired goods are scarce the distribution is not satisfactory, that is, either the distribution is equitable and does not fully satisfy anyone's desire, or the distribution is inequitable and satisfies some to the detriment of others. But since the legitimization of this distributive practice was part of an institutional process which was equitable for the whole human community or for a group, the cause of the non-satisfaction was not explained in individual terms which were humiliating. We can say that the explanation was presented in collective terms. For instance, a person who could not have access to a good because belonging to an inferior caste did not have the feeling of personal failure, to the extent that the non-satisfaction was not a personal problem, but rather a problem of his caste, as a whole.

It is clear that this solution does not eliminate the problem of justice

---

23 On mimetic desire and violence, see Girard, *Violence and the Sacred*.

24 René Girard, *El misterio de nuestro mundo*, Salamanca, Sígueme, 1982, p. 328. [English language edn: *Things Hidden since the Foundation of the World*, trans. Stephen Bann and Michael Metteer, London, The Athlone Press, 1987.]

in the process of distribution of the desired goods, but the feeling of failure does not fall on the individual. In these societies, due to the absence of the myth of infinite progress one has more clearly the notion of limits, and that leads them to create, even if unconsciously, the mechanisms of control of the mimetic desires.

In modern societies with the myth of progress, mimetic desires rather than being repressed are encouraged. Furthermore, in their struggle to conquer the earthly paradise or the kingdom of freedom,

> modern people always imagine that their ills and disgraces come from the hindrances that the religious taboos and cultural interdicts place in the desire; and in our days from the legal protections of the judicial systems. Once these barriers are put down they think that one can expand the desire and that its marvellous innocence will, at last, produce fruits.[25]

It is to this basic difference between these two types of society that Koetler referred in a passage already referred to: 'Those in less developed [premodern] societies will try to reduce or satisfy their desires with what is available', while 'those who belong to industrialized societies will try to find or develop objects that will satisfy their desires'.[26]

Thus, there are no more cultural interdicts, or better said, the interdicts are reversed, and ironically, now they encourage mimetic desire. Because of this, the frustration of not being able to obey the social imperative of fulfilling their desire – a frustration from which a part of society cannot escape according to the logic of mimetic desire – is explained in individual terms. Then, the 'frustrated' individual (in our case the poor in the capitalist society) internalizes the guilt feeling for the failure. He perceives his situation as the fruit of his culpability rather than as the necessary consequence of an adopted model of development. Therefore he cannot rebel against this same model that he continues to see as the only way to fulfil, perhaps in the future, his mimetic desires.

When a major part of society no longer accepts either the delay in fulfilling the promises or the individual blaming of the poor and proposes a more class-based vision of the problem, demanding either a sharing in the benefits of progress or the immediate satisfaction of needs and desires, we have the exhaustion of capitalist legitimization

---

25 Girard, *El misterio*, p. 323.
26 See footnote 5.

as analysed above. In more serious cases, in view of a possible violent irruption of a crisis, the dominant sectors of society may (and usually do) adopt violent measures to control the situation.

In the decade of the 1970s the illusions of the myth of development began to collapse. In 1972 a report sponsored by the Club of Rome, *The Limits to Growth*[27] showed that if the pace of economic growth and the level of consumption of the First World expanded worldwide we would have economic chaos due to the crisis of non-renewable resources and environmental pollution. In 1973 we had the oil crisis as an almost historical corroboration of the wake-up calls from that report. This enhanced world awareness regarding an objective fact: it is not possible to satisfy everyone's mimetic desires. In 1982 we had the beginnings of the external debt crisis, and the 'lost decade' with the structural adjustments imposed by the IMF and the World Bank.[28]

With the awareness of the limits of the economic growth and the resulting social problems resulting from the hard measures of economic adjustments imposed in the name of the market laws, the controlling mechanism (based only on the promise of postponing the fulfillment of desires) became ineffective. In other words, a violent external mechanism became necessary to control a possible violence born out of the frustration of a desire encouraged by society's own mechanisms. No longer would people agree voluntarily to control their wish to satisfy their basic needs and mimetic desires.

Thus we have the virulent appearance of what was already latent (or present in a timid way): the argument of the 'necessary sacrifices for progress'[29] claimed by the market laws. If, in the dynamic of the mimetic desire, progress is the result of competition and the law of the survival of the most competent, then we have here a logical deduction: the sacrifice of the less competent becomes a necessity in the dynamics of progress itself. We have here a third hypothesis.

The problem lies in that mimetic desire's incentive in a stagnant or low economic growth situation generates a crisis – where people no longer respect the established rules to make their desires come true – if the self-controlling mechanism based on the postponing of promises does not function. Thus to the argument of necessary sacrifices is added

---

27 D. H. Meadows, D. L. Meadows, J. Randers and W. Beherens III, *Limits to Growth*, New York, Universe Books, 1974.

28 On the external debt crisis and its relationship with theology, see Jung Mo Sung, *A idolatria do capital e a morte dos pobres*, 2nd edn, S. Paulo, Paulinas, 1991, and F. Hinkelammert, *La deuda externa de America Latina*, San José, DEI, 1989.

29 Mário Henrique Simonsen, *Brasil 2000*, 6th edn, Rio de Janeiro, APEC, 1976, p. 28.

that of keeping under control this contradiction of the mimetic logic so as to prevent a more serious crisis. The discourse of necessary sacrifices is effective also because the poor have internalized the previously described guilt feelings. As such they agree to be victims of necessary sacrifices. On the opposite side, this provides relief of conscience to the sacrifice demanders or beneficiaries of the sacrificial mechanism. Galbraith, analysing the 'culture of contentment' that exists in our societies, says that those in this sector perceive their benefits as 'just deserts' and that 'if good fortune is deserved or is a reward of personal merit, there is no credible justification for any action that could come to damage or inhibit it – that comes to reduce what is or might be able to be enjoyed'[30]. The other side of the coin in this vision is that the poor are deserving of the sacrifices imposed on them. This is a theology of retribution.

The talk by economists and politicians of necessary sacrifices brings to light the problem of secularization of modern society.[31] It is not possible to discuss this theme in the context of this work. Yet to comprehend the depth of this logic of necessary sacrifices for maximizing progress and, therefore, for reaching paradise, and, at the same time, as necessary for the stability of the social order, we need to go beyond the naive view that with the secularization of modern societies we no longer have the presence of the sacred in the public, political and economic spheres.

The fact that traditional religions are no longer the foundation of the social order does not necessarily mean that the new foundation will not claim for itself characteristics previously attributed to the religious and sacred spheres. This becomes clearer if we take into account that one of the fundamental characteristics of modernity is the making immanent of medieval eschatology. In other words, the paradise previously expected to come by divine action mediated through the Church, is now expected to come as a result of progress. In the capitalist world this redeeming progress is expected to come about through the market. That is why the market, the new foundation of society, claims for itself (or as ardent defenders attribute to it) the characteristic of the sacred.

In this sense the process of secularization cannot be understood as the elimination of the sacred, as the desacralization of society,

---

30 John Kenneth Galbraith, *The Culture of Contentment*, New York and Boston, Houghton Mifflin, 1992, pp. 18–19.

31 Giacomo Marramao, *Céu e Terra: genealogia da secularização*, São Paulo, Ed. Unesp, 1997; *Poder e secularização: as categorias do tempo*, São Paulo, UNESP, 1995; Stefano Martelli, *A religião na sociedade pós-modernas: entre secularização e dessecularização*, São Paulo, Paulinas, 1995.

but rather as the relocation of the sacred from the Church, from the traditional religious sphere, to the market. That is the reason why today the speech of necessary sacrifices is more associated with the economic rather than with the traditional religious field. In Chapter 1 we had a small example of how capitalist economic talk is full of religious logic and terminology, which turn these sacrifices into truly religious sacrifices.[32]

Yet, René Girard, himself a great scholar of violence and the sacred, conceives the secularization of modern society in terms of desacralization and for that reason he says that this violence, contrary to archaic violence, no longer utilizes the sacrificial mechanism to overcome its crisis. He believes that the modern judicial system replaced in a more effective way the sacrificial system. The problem is that modern capitalist societies encourage mimetic desires, and this poses the big challenge of maintaining order in the face of the permanent threats of conflicts that they generate. Before proceeding, it is important to say that, as Girard showed in his studies of archaic societies, the sacrificial system is effective in maintaining the social order to the extent that the sacrificial society is unaware of its mechanism. Thus we can say that the sacrificial mechanism we are considering here derives its effectiveness in maintaining social order (based in the encouragement of the mimetic desire) precisely from the lack of awareness of most people regarding this mechanism. It is unawareness at such a level as to prevent people from even admitting the existence of sacrificial mechanisms. Another important point regarding its effectiveness is the 'certainty' of the culpability of the victims, whether by the members of the sacrificial system or by the sacrificed ones themselves.

In defending the idea that the capitalist system utilizes sacrificial mechanisms we do not mean that such mechanisms are equal to those of archaic societies. Certainly there is a distinctive character in the sacrificial violence of modernity.[33] With Christianity a radically new notion was introduced in the West, that is the notion of a world where there is no longer scarcity, and for that reason all desires are satis-

---

32 On theology inside the economic speech see, for instance, J. M. Sung, *Deus numa economia sem coração*; Hugo Assmann, *Desafios e falácias*, São Paulo, Paulinas, 1992; F. Hinkelammert, *As armas ideológicas da morte*, São Paulo, Paulinas, 1983.

33 The author who influenced me most in the elaboration of this thinking about the sacrificial violence of modernity was Franz Hinkelammert. It is worthy mentioning his work *Sacrifícios humanos y sociedad occidental? Lucifer y la Bestia*, San José, DEI, 1991; also the work of H. Assmann and E. Hinkelammert, *Idolatria do mercado*, Petrópolis, Vozes, 1989. On the sacrificial utopia of modernity, see also: J. M. Sung, *Teologia e economia*, ch. IV.

fied (paradise) and, therefore, sacrifices are no longer necessary. Thus appears the notion of the 'final sacrifice', the sacrifice of Jesus, and the notion of society without sacrifices. We cannot forget that this notion is present during the transition from premodern to modern societies. Thus the notion of sacrifice is still a ritual and religious one.

The problem is that in spite of this doctrine of paradise on the horizon of the historical future, societies continue having the challenge of scarcity and unsatisfied mimetic desires. Now, instead of reaching back to the mechanism of archaic societies and reproducing the sacrifice ritual around a scapegoat, what happens is a reformulation of the notion of sacrifice. The postponing of the Parousia is blamed on the existence of heathens who still celebrate sacrifices and do not accept the definitive sacrifice of Jesus, and, more importantly, on the sins of the sacrificers of Jesus. Thus one pursues the obligatory conversion of all heathens and sacrifices the sacrificers in order to hasten the arrival of paradise. Now sacrifice is not to curb and control the mimetic desires, but to make them come true.

In modernity the way to paradise showed up as technical-economic progress. The incentive of mimetic desire demands more sacrifices in order to maintain the stability of an order that exists in permanent instability and crisis by its own dynamic of progress–desire–mimetic desire. Now the sacrifice of the less competent, of those excluded from the economic dynamic, is a necessity related to progress; ditto of the sacrifice of those who do not submit themselves to market laws, those trying to obtain the necessary living goods without respect for private property or the buying–selling relationship. Finally also sacrificed must be those who do not accept the sacredness of, and pretend to intervene in, the market in the name of social goals and social justice. For as Girard says, 'the function of sacrifice is to quell violence within the community and to prevent conflicts from erupting'.[34]

The hunger and death of millions of the poor, all over Latin America and other countries of the Third World, are sacrifices that should ensure that further sacrifices will no longer be needed. The slandering and persecutions of defenders of rights and dignity of the poor are part of this sacrificial process.

Taboos and human dignity

One of the most important characteristics of the premodern religious sacrificial solution is the elaboration of taboos that rule the actions of

---

34 Girard, *Violence and the Sacred*, p. 14.

members of the community, thus forbidding the desire for objects that can generate mimetic crisis. The classic example of taboo is incest. This taboo is a good example to help us perceive that taboos also are useful in differentiating humans from 'monsters'. Even today it is common to hear of people who disregarded such fundamental taboos being referred to as 'monsters'. The opposite is also true: when society, or some group, wants to purge persons or groups, without a reasonable justification, it is customary for the former first to attribute to the latter the crime of incest or some other perversion, namely the crime of those who disregard taboo. Those who do not obey the taboos are not human, and therefore have no human rights or human dignity.

As we saw before, in modern capitalist society the mimetic desire generated by the market is *encouraged* desire. This does not mean that there are no taboos any more. They still exist, in order for the mimetic desires to persist. But they take another form. Now, not all taboos are the prohibitive 'you may not!' Many come with the obligatory 'you must!' The most well-known inversion is the one of the sexual taboo. From the 'you may not', we came to the 'you must'. In the field of the economy, without doubt, the taboo is 'buy'! , 'buy the famous brand'!

Nizan Guanaes, director of a great publicity agency, wrote that 'Nike is not a tennis shoe, but rather a life model. Nike is a style and a vision of the world.' His announcements are evangelical. They not only sell, they indoctrinate. They not only convince, they convert. For him, Nike transforms people, makes them feel themselves as their own idols for wearing Nike. 'Nike makes the boy from the Third World feel so good, as if he were sniffing glue. That is why many boys who could not have Nike do have Nike. Because if he cannot have it he dies'.[35] Thus, we can add that there are many street children who kill to get Nike, and others who would rather risk their lives than go out without their Nike.

'Buy Nike', like any other brand that is in fashion and that is an object of mimetic desire, became a condition for belonging to the human community. By doing that, people are not really buying a pair of tennis-shoes but rather striving for 'being' the kind of persons who would obtain recognition in their relationships with other members of the community living under this taboo. Thus, Nike is not merely an object of desire. It became a need. Finally we have arrived at the knot of the confusion between the concept of need and desire, as well as to the mysterious passage from desire to need, as mentioned by Hayek.

---

35 'Nike é um estilo e uma visão do mundo', *Folha de S. Paulo* (4 Feb. 1994), pp. 2–4.

We must differentiate objective needs for the reproduction of our bodily life from the needs interjected by taboo and mimetic desire, which are conditions for one to belong in society or in any social group. No one dies for not having a Nike, but dies indeed without eating and drinking, whether or not one wishes to. The extreme condition of anorexia helps us see the difference between real need and desire transformed into need due to cultural (taboos) or psychic problems.

One of the aspects of the relation between need and desire is the relation between object or desired objective and the condition of possibility to achieve it. 'I want to be accepted by this group and for that I need to have an imported pair of tennis-shoes;' the fact of one having a pair of imported tennis-shoes does not necessarily mean belonging to the group, but rather the condition of possibility, because this is a precondition established by the group in question.

When we talk of need as condition of possibility, we must differentiate two types of need: the 'basic' and the 'social or psychic'. The first condition for any person to wish something and to fight for it is to be alive. A dead person is not a subject, and even less a subject of desire. This means that the satisfaction of basic needs, which makes one's survival possible, is the primary condition. It is the type of need that popular and church-related movements highlight. But beyond being alive persons must feel themselves 'alive', that is, as belonging to a social group, as being recognized as persons by other persons. And here comes the 'social and psychic need', referred to by Hayek and the marketing people.

Desire is what moves people and makes them reach for energies for struggling. Desire attracts us while needs, especially basic needs, push us.

The other point that we should reaffirm is the 'mystical character' of commodities in our societies. It is what Marx called the 'fetishism of commodities'. It is due to the mysterious and infinite 'being' one tries to find, for instance, behind an imported car, a great object of mimetic desire, that people neither accept nor understand the need for income redistribution or profound structural reforms. And the poor who do not manage either to buy or to overcome this mystique of the commodity are left with the feeling of being less, of being inferior, of being guilty, without dignity, and, therefore, even without the right to fight.

Against the violent 'monsters', that is the poor who do not buy famous name brand commodities and who want to satisfy their basic needs without obeying the taboo of private property and the laws of the market – society, namely those integrated into the market and who internalize these taboos, feels itself just in the use of all forms of legal (or even illegal) violence, since they are 'legitimate', according to the spirit of the market.

Challenges for Christianity

The struggle for the life of the poor and the excluded from our societies demands urgent income and wealth redistribution, a change in the productive system aiming at a better income distribution, and profound reforms of the economic, social and political structure. But to accomplish this it is fundamental to unmask the sacrificial mechanism of mimetic desire. Otherwise it would be very difficult to set the satisfaction of basic needs of the whole population as a priority of economic policy. I do not want to deny the role of desire, but only to re-establish common sense in the social dynamic.

Premodern societies utilized religious taboos to tame the mimetic desires that could place at risk the integrity of the community as a whole. Today, in modern societies this is no longer possible or desirable, theologically speaking. Desire is part and parcel of the human being and has a mimetic dynamic. This means that the mimetic character of consumption, one of the causes of our dualism, cannot be eliminated by any decree or revolution. If the construction of a wholly new society based in wholly new men and women were possible, maybe we could think of an economy without the problem of mimetic consumption. But since this absolutely new reality is not historically possible, we must learn to deal with the mimetic desire of appropriation as an anthropological and social component.

A possible way for us to deal with this process is the unmasking, the revealing, of the sacrificial mechanism hidden under our consumption-exacerbated culture. And from there the establishing, through democratic mechanisms and new social covenants, of economic policies and laws that would set limits to the satisfaction of desires for luxury consumer goods that hinder the economic development for the whole population.

It is fundamental that we tame the mimetic desire of appropriation so as to make room for consensus or majority support for this kind of society, a basic condition for democracy. In capitalism the desire for having has become not only central but also almost total. Even in personal relationships 'persons are transformed into things; their relations with each other assume the character of ownership'.[36]

---

36 Erich Fromm, *To Have or to Be?* New York, Harper & Row, 1976, p. 71.

The taming of the mimetic desire of appropriation does not mean wishing to finish with it, but rather limiting it by highlighting another type of mimetic desire, namely, the desire to be like the persons that we assume as our model or master. In Girard's terminology this is the mimetic desire of representation. For the logic of possessing to be tamed by the logic of being, or even better, lest the being be pursued only in the having, one must establish the difference between these two logics. As Fromm says, 'the difference between having and being is not essentially that between East or West. The difference is rather between a society centered on persons and one centered on things'.[37]

So that the human and qualitative dimensions of life become worthier in society; so that the desire may not be channelled only to the having, but also and mainly to the being (as persons who discovered the human meaning of life), we need, as Leonardo Boff reminds us, exemplary characters such as St Francis of Assisi. They are 'like mirrors in which the dreams that encourage practice and the values that nurture great motivations are convincingly reflected and provide us meaning to live, suffer, fight and hope'.[38] We need people [like that] who in solidarity and encounter and communion with the poor and with nature lived out the 'relinquishing of the instinct of possession'.[39]

To prioritize some social objectives we need, besides the differentiation of the concepts of need and desire, the re-establishing of a truth, namely, the innocence of the victims. If Christianity still has any historical relevance and anything to contribute toward the construction of an alternative society in Latin America, it must be anchored on the very centre of our faith: the resurrection of Jesus, which at the bottom is the confession of the innocence of a victim of a sacrificial system. In line with that, Hugo Assmann said that 'the essential novelty of the Christian message . . . consists in the central affirmation that the victims are innocent and that no excuse or pretext justifies their victimization',[40] and that this central element of our faith compels us to an attitude of solidarity with all the victims around us.

The defence of the victims of the sacrifices demanded by the market system makes it possible for us to unmask the sacrificial system and

---

37 Fromm, *To Have or to Be?*, p. 19.

38 Leonardo Boff, *Ecologia: grito da Terra, grito dos pobres*, São Paulo, Ática, 1995, p. 310. [English language edn: *Cry of the Earth, Cry of the Poor*, Maryknoll, NY, Orbis Books, 1997.]

39 Boff, *Ecologia*, p. 310

40 Hugo Assmann, 'The strange imputation of violence to Liberation Theology', Conference on Religion and Violence, New York, 12–15 Oct. 1989, in *Terrorism and Political Violence*, vol. 3, n. 4 (Winter 1991), London, Frank Cass, pp. 84–5.

see not only the perversity of the market laws but also the responsibility of all those who benefit from the market and adore it. For only a transcendentalized institution (idol) could demand so many human sacrifices in the name of a future paradise and generate such a tranquil conscience in its worshippers and defenders.

To be on the side of the victims, helping them rebuild their denied human dignity, allows us to see – because it makes possible an epistemological revolution – that God 'desires mercy, not sacrifice' (Matt. 9.13); that we do become more human not in the buying of commodities that others also desire, but rather in solidarity with our brethren; and that sin consists precisely in the fulfilment of the (market's) Law.[41]

We will not be able to deeply transform our unjust economic and social structures without the participation of important sectors of society, involving many people. To that end we need to help them go beyond the logic of the market's mimetic desire and sacrificial mechanism. We need to help them discover the innocence of our economy's sacrificial victims and help them pursue an alternative way to live their lives and to relate themselves in society. Thus, together we will be constructing a new project of society and civilization. I believe that we Christians do have a significant role to play regarding this historical challenge. After all, our faith springs from the affirmation of the innocence of the victim of a sacrificial system and a sacrificial god.

---

41 For the fundamental question of law and sin in Saint Paul, see Elsa Tamez, *Contra Toda Condone*, San José, DEI, 1991.

3

The Contribution of Theology in the Struggle against Social Exclusion

Social exclusion

Microprocessors the size of a credit card with one quarter of a billion transistors and computers based on optoelectronics and responsive to oral command; transmission and information mechanisms whose speed is measured in trillions of *bits* (the smallest measure of information) a second; a dense global meganet of fibre optics, satellite connections, wireless links and circuits of digital images surrounding the planet. These are some of the accelerators of change in our civilization. High technology and the process of globalization of the economy are creating a new face for the world.

Meanwhile the UN informs us that the population in extreme poverty reached one billion and three hundred million in 1995 (two thirds of which are women). One in five persons in the world suffers 'debilitating poverty' and survives with less than a dollar a day; more than one billion people are in need of basic services; one in 100 people is an immigrant or refugee, and one in four adults is illiterate. In a planet that avidly consumes virtual realities, every day one fifth of the population has nothing to eat, while eight hundred billion dollars – equalling the income of half of the world population – are yearly spent in military programmes.

This blatant contrast is a small picture of our time. It is a time that can be characterized by those who have not yet lost their capacity for ethical indignation, as an 'epoch of perplexity'.[1]

It is clear that the newness of our time lies neither in the continuity of the social contrasts nor in their deepening, but rather, as Hugo Assmann says, '*the major fact* in the world's current conjuncture is certainly the frightening empire of the logic of exclusion and the

---

1 René A. Dreyfus, *A época das perplexidades. Mundialização, globalização e planetarização: novos desafios*, Petrópolis, Vozes, 1996.

growing insensitivity of too many in relation to it'.[2] The promise of a rich world without social inequalities brought about by liberal thinking with its myth of development[3] reflected in their theories of development turned out to be unfeasible and fallacious. Neoliberalism, today's dominant ideology, no longer has the concern of presenting itself as the bearer of solution for social problems of the population as a whole, that is, they do not defend equality as a value to be materialized. In the words of Cristovam Buarque,

> as long as the world was physically divided one could bear the idea of equality without practising it. . . . Once the world is integrated by the communication and transportation, by the economy and migrations that interlink the people, the poor come physically and in consumption desires closer to the rich, but socially they become even more separated; the egalitarian speech turns out contradictory.[4]

That being the case, neoliberals explicitly assume social inequality as a value or as an inescapable fact and develop a culture of insensibility.

The new reality of social exclusion, or *social apartheid*, introduces a new dialectic in society. Alongside the old dialectic of capital versus labour, one needs also to think of the dichotomy of those integrated in the market and those excluded as well as the compassionate, that is those dissatisfied with the current excluding logic.[5] And this phenomenon of social exclusion is not exclusive to Third or Fourth World

---

2 Hugo Assmann, 'Por una sociedad donde quepan todos', in José Duque (ed.), *Por una sociedad donde quepan todos* (Quarta Jornada Teológica de CETELA, 10–13 July 1995), San José (Costa Rica), DEI, 1996, pp. 379–92. Quoted on p. 380.

3 Celso Furtado, *O mito do desenvolvimento econômico*, Rio de Janeiro, Paz e Terra, 1974. See also Jung Mo Sung, *Teologia e economia*, 2nd edn, Petrópolis, Vozes, 1995, chs. IV and V.

4 Cristovam Buarque, 'O pensamento em um mundo . . .', in Marcel Bursztyn (ed.), *Para pensar o desenvolvimento sustentável*, São Paulo, Brasiliense, 1993, pp. 57–80. Quoted on p. 70.

5 J. K. Galbraith, *A sociedade justa: uma perspectiva humana*, Rio de Janeiro, Campus, 1966, says: 'The old dichotomy [capitalist vs. workers] survives in the public psyche – the residue of its long and ardent history. Yet, in the economy and in modern States, the division is rather different, and this happens in all economically advanced nations. On the one hand, now there are the rich, the comfortably installed and those that aim at being so; and on the other, those economically less fortunate and the poor alongside a considerable number that, either due to concern or sympathy aim at speaking on their behalf or for a more compassionate world. This is the current economic and political line-up' (p. 8). [English language edn: *The Good Society: The Humane Agenda*, Wilmington, Mass., Houghton Mifflin, 1996.]

countries. It is also part of the rich countries. The difference is that in poor countries there are minorities who live in big pockets of wealth in the midst of the poor majority, while in the rich countries the big pockets of poverty constitute the minority part.

The role of theology

Before continuing with the reflection on the fundamental problem of social exclusion, we need to focus for a while on the role of theology in the current socio-economic situation. We will approach this issue from the standpoint of two questions: a) Should theology and the Christian churches assume these macro-economic-social concerns? b) if yes, is the theological speech about this theme addressed only to the Christian communities and people interested in the attitude of Christians, or has it a real relevance for the ongoing debate about this in the academic and political world?

Religion and politics

Regarding the first question, there is already a sufficient number of books and articles on the social and political implications of faith which show that we cannot reduce the Christian faith to the boundaries of the personal and interpersonal spheres. Neither can we reduce theological reflection to inter-ecclesial problems, such as faith education of the members of the community, or the relationship between community life and the needed secular activities (for instance, administration of church properties).

Yet, this response does not exhaust our question. This is so because it is customary for us to find in the midst of Christian groups committed to action in solidarity with the excluded or with the struggles of women, indigenous and Black people, the influence of postmodern thinking with its valorization of the fragment, the particular, and the daily perspective, to the detriment of a thinking able to encompass a comprehensive concept of social and strategic action. In practice this almost means the exclusive valorization of local and specific works without linkage with more comprehensive social and political projects. I am not trying to deny here the importance of concrete and localized efforts but rather trying to show that these types of effort, which express the 'option for the poor', do not necessarily imply the articulation of faith with the great social questions and projects.

Actually, it is not uncommon to hear in theological or pastoral situations people previously committed to the transformation of society now saying that we should not think about possible alternatives, but only about concrete actions of solidarity. Others say that we should abandon theology as a rational speech and assume it as an exclusively aesthetic-poetic one unrelated to possible contributions to social changes.

We perceive, as Boaventura dos Santos says that 'the difficulty in accepting or suffering the injustices and irrationalities of the capitalist society hinders rather than enhances the possibility of thinking of a society totally distinct and better than this one'.[6] This is because 'the new contextualism and particularism make it difficult for one to think strategically of emancipation. Local struggles and contextual identities tend to favour tactical rather than strategic thinking'.[7] It is important to note that the globalization of capital happens simultaneously with the localization of labour as well as with the valorization of private and contextualized struggles. The crisis of strategic and emancipatory thinking does not necessarily mean a crisis of principles which stand for the dignity of all human beings or, in theological terms, for the option for the poor. Rather than a crisis of principles, it seems to be a crisis of social actors interested in the application of these principles, and also a crisis of model societies where such principles can materialize.

Besides this difficulty, there is another fundamental question raised by José Comblin, in his latest book, *Cristãos Rumo ao Século XXI: Nova Caminhada de Libertação* (*Christians Bound for the 21st Century: A New Journey of Liberation*). According to him, the participation of the churches in the struggle for the solution of the social problems that afflict our people has not meant the overcoming of the dichotomy between religion and politics. For many there remains the dualism between religious and social doctrines, between salvation and human promotion/liberation. 'One professes that the former is immutable and fixed doctrine, while the other is enriched with the emerging of new social situations that create new challenges and new answers,'[8] It is 'a dualism in the gospel from which Liberation Theology does not escape'.[9] He adds that

> There is no more urgent task than the one of reuniting once again what was separated for so long, the 'political' and the 'religious', the

---

6 Boaventura Sousa Santos, *Pela mão de Alice: o social e o político na pós-modernidade*, São Paulo, Cortez, 1995, p. 147.

7 Santos, *Pela mão de Alice*, p. 147.

8 José Comblin, *Cristãos rumo ao século XXI: nova caminhada de libertação*, São Paulo, Paulus, 1996, p. 98.

9 Comblin, *Cristãos rumo*, p. 97.

'social' and the 'mystic'. It is a practical rather than a theoretical task, although theory has to contribute to anchor and to orient an effective practice.[10]

In quoting Comblin's text, we do not mean to agree fully with his sweeping statement, rather we need to understand that there still is progress to be made in theological reflection about and from the standpoint of political and economic practices, problems and challenges, and that must be done in dialogue with other branches of knowledge that address these questions.

Summarizing, we should continue confronting two theoretical/practical challenges, namely, a) to develop a strategic thinking capable of articulating local and particular actions with a more encompassing long-term project; b) to improve our theological speech about the relationship between salvation and human promotion/liberation.

Specific contribution of theology

With that in mind, let's go to the second question. What is the target audience of theological reflection? It is clear that it is primarily the theological community itself and the communities of the faithful (the Christian people and the hierarchy). This is more than obvious. Therefore, at the bottom, the question is whether theology has a relevant and specific contribution to make to the ongoing debate about economic and social questions carried out outside the church's domain, namely, in the academic and political areas, and in social movements. In other words, is there, in the debate about the formulation and construction of another model of society anything that has specifically to do with theology to the point that if theology did not come in with its reflection the whole effort would be weakened? Or is it that the only function of theological reflection about social problems and possible alternatives is the one of encouraging and 'orienting' the Christians to participate in this struggle?

I am fully aware that the answer to this question demands much more than the few lines of this text.[11] However, due to its relevance, one has to pursue it, even if confined to given limitations and possibilities. Marx begins the text which contains the famous saying 'religion is

---

10 Comblin, *Cristãos rumo*, p. 105.

11 I dealt, partially, with this question in my book *Teologia e economia: repensando a TL e utopias*. See also H. Assmann and F. Hinkelammert, *Idolatria do mercado*, Petrópolis, Vozes, 1989.

the opium of the people' stating: 'For Germany the *criticism of religion is in the main complete, and the criticism of religion is the premise of all criticism*'.[12] In other words, without the desacralizing of the status quo one cannot pursue any critique. This affirmation by Marx continues to be valid even today. The mistake is to believe that with the secularization of modern societies the process of sacralization or naturalization of society, which in our case is the market system, does not exist any more.

Secularization did not mean the end of the gods and religions, but rather the replacement of God's sovereignty as the foundation of society and of eschatological promises by the notion of popular sovereignty, and later, by the notion of economic rationality of the market as the foundation of society and the promises of the myth of progress. The utopia of eschatological hope of the Middle Ages was secularized and transformed in a utopian opening of the horizon of expectation based on the concept of progress. As G. Marramao says, 'the innovating result whence flows the process of secularization in eighteenth-century Europe is the transformation of eschatology into utopia: planning history becomes as important as conquering nature. The mechanics or inner logic of this transformation is fully transposed to the new philosophy of history centered in the concept of *progress*'.[13] With this, 'paradise' was relocated from the after-death transcendence to the future in the interior of history, thus bringing to an end the notion of limits to human action.

It is this revolution in the conception of time, history and human possibilities that makes possible and comprehensible affirmations such as the following by George Gilder criticizing intellectuals for confronting capitalism with the problem of ecology and non-renewable resources: 'man is not finite';[14] or by Fukuyama who says that capitalism with its 'technology makes possible the limitless accumulation of wealth, and thus the satisfaction of an ever-expanding set of human desires'.[15] Neoliberal thinking, as we saw above, abandoned the idea that all equally can and should participate in this limitless satisfaction

---

12 'Contribution to the Critique of Hegel's Philosophy of Right. Introduction', in K. Marx and F. Engels, *On Religion*, Moscow, Progress Publishers, 1972, p. 37. Final sequence of italics is ours.

13 Giacomo Marramao, *Poder e secularização: as categorias do tempo*, São Paulo, UNESP, 1995, p. 103.

14 George Gilder, *O Espírito da Empresa*, São Paulo, Pionneira, 1989, p. 61. [English language edn: *The Spirit of Enterprise*, New York, Simon & Schuster, 1984.]

15 F. Fukuyama, *The End of History and the Last Man*, New York, N.Y., The Free Press, 1992, p. xiv. (Italics ours.)

of desires, but did not abandon this possibility for the winners in the market competition.

This mythic vision of the capacity of the market system and technology to enhance the limitless accumulation of wealth and to fulfil all human desires has two fundamental problems. The first is the negation of the limits of natural resources and the ecological system. Such limits would reveal the impossibility of limitless accumulation.[16] The second is the notion of desire reduced to relation of subject and object of desire plus the scarcity of goods as the only obstacle to the satisfaction of all desires. When Fukuyama associates limitless accumulation with satisfaction of the always growing set of human desires, he reduces the structure of human desire to the subject and object relation and explains scarcity only as the result of the lack of technical development and the lack of full implementation of the capitalist system.[17] Yet, he himself acknowledges that the structure of desire is not simply reduced to the relation between subject and object of desire. Anchoring himself on Hegel, he says that humans as animals do have natural needs and desires for external objects such as eating, drinking and sheltering, and also that 'man differs fundamentally from the animals . . . because . . . he desires the desire of other men, that is, he wants to be "recognized". In particular he wants to be recognized as a *human being*, that is, as a being with a certain worth or dignity.'[18] And in the pursuit of recognition 'man derives satisfaction owning property not only for the needs that it satisfies, but because other men recognize it. [. . .] Hegel sees property as a stage or aspect of the historical struggle for recognition, as something that satisfies *thymos* [the psychological place of desire and self-recognition], as well as desire.'[19].

Why is it that the possession of a certain property leads to recognition by the other? This is a question that Fukuyama does not raise, but it is important that we raise it here. A very plausible answer is that ownership of a certain good generates recognition, because the other who recognizes it also desires and appreciates this property. Therefore, if I want to be recognized the thing to do is to desire and possess the object desired by the other person so that this other person will recognize me. This is what Girard calls the mimetic desire of appropriation.

It is obvious that the desire of recognition is restricted neither to the

16 The Club of Rome report, *The Limits to the Growth*, 1972, already called attention to such limits.

17 See F. Fukuyama, *End of History*, p. xi.

18 Fukuyama, *End of History*, p. xvi.

19 Fukuyama, *End of History*, p. 195.

economic field nor to the ownership of material goods. In Girardian terms we could say that the pursuit of recognition could happen through the mimetism of appropriation or representation. But, as Fukuyama himself recognizes, in capitalist societies the emphasis is almost exclusively on the mimetic desire of appropriation. That is why he says that the struggle for recognition previously waged in the 'military, religious or nationalist plan is now fought in the economic plan. The princes that in other times strove to defeat each other, risking their lives in bloody battles, now risk their capital, building industrial empires.'[20] With this,

> what generally is taken as economic motivations is not, in fact, a question of rational desire, but a manifestation of the desire of recognition. The natural desires and needs are few and easily satisfied, particularly in the context of a modern industrial economy. Our motivation to work and make money is intimately related to the recognition that this activity gives us an activity in which the money becomes a symbol not of material goods, but of social status or recognition.[21]

If the human being pursues recognition, by desiring the desire of the other human beings and their models, namely, if the desire is mimetic, this human being will not be able to fulfil all the desires through the limitless accumulation of goods, even if such limitless accumulation were possible.

This is so because the basic structure of mimetic desire consists in that I desire an object not for the object in itself, but for the fact that another person desires it. That being the case, the object desired by both is always scarce in relation to the subjects of the desire. It is because it is scarce that it is the object of desire. Thus a rivalry is created between the two who desire the same object. This rivalry, or conflict, has the modern name of competition. Liberal economists call this competition the mover of progress. Furthermore, since in the dynamic of the capitalist economy, as usual, there are always novelties as objects of desire, scarcity (always related to desire) is a basic fact. Thus, the resulting rivalry and violence become endemic, always present.

The contradiction or the insufficiency in Fukuyama's thinking happens because he deals at the same time with two conflictive notions

---

20 F. Fukuyama, *Confiança: as virtudes sociais e a criação da prosperidade*, Rio de Janeiro, Rocco, 1996, p. 381. [English language edn: *Trust: The Social Virtues and the Creation of Prosperity*, New Jersey, The Free Press, 1996.]
21 Fukuyama, *Confiança*, pp. 379–80.

about desire, that is, the desire for objects and mimetic desire. This comes from his defending at the same time the market system and liberal democracy as ways for satisfying two desires: the accumulation of goods (desire for objects) and recognition, which according to him, would be fulfilled by liberal democracy. Behind this model is the illusion or modern myth of the possibility of the satisfaction of all our desires.

Since he does not want to renounce this myth, he separates two kinds of desire: the limitless desire for objects, which could be satisfied with the limitless accumulation of wealth; and the desire of recognition, which would have the mimetic structure. The problem is that with this kind of separation he cannot explain why people desire some objects that are not necessary for their survival and why they desire them in a limitless way.

René Girard explained this question in a more precise form by saying that

> [O]nce his basic needs are satisfied (indeed, sometimes even before), man is subject to intense desires, though he may not know precisely for what. The reason is that he desires *being*, something he himself lacks and which some other person seems to possess. The subject thus looks to that other person to inform him of what he should desire in order to acquire that being. If the model, who is apparently already endowed with superior being, desires some object, that object must surely be capable of conferring an even greater plenitude of being. It is not through words, therefore, but by the example of his own desire that the model conveys to the subject the supreme desirability of the object.[22]

Hayek, as we saw in the previous chapter, in dealing with the theme of desire and economic progress solved this question in a better way than Fukuyama. For him mimetic desire is the mover of economic progress because by the dynamic of the same progress the benefits of new learning can be made available only gradually. It is the mimetic desire of the majority of the population that, in trying to imitate the consumption of the elite, will demand more technological advances and direct economic production toward the satisfaction of this desire of imitative consumption.

There is a certain determinism in this theory of the technological

---

22 René Girard, *Violence and the Sacred*, Baltimore and London, Johns Hopkins University Press, 1979, p. 146.

advance and the directing of production. It is due to the fact that for Hayek

> a new good or new commodity, before becoming a *public need* and part of life's need they 'constitute usually the fancy of some few chosen ones'. 'The luxuries of today are the needs of tomorrow.' Even more: the new things or new goods . . . turn out to become the patrimony of the majority just *because* for a while they were the luxury of the minority.[23]

Here we have the transition of the desire from 'today's luxury' (superfluous goods, as some would say) to public needs brought about by the dynamic of the mimetic desire. It is the pursuit of being in the desire of having what the model, the elite, desires and has. It generates this transition from desire to public or social need. Thus, we cannot separate so radically objects of desire (seen as superfluous) from objects of need (seen as basic necessities), because over the minimum limit of biological survival, the 'social' needs are determined by the process of imitation of the desire of the social model.

Here one must introduce the problem of discerning between the desired licit and the desired illicit objects, or the 'control' of desires. According to Hayek, 'every progressive society, while resting on the mentioned process of learning and imitation, only admits the desires that it creates as incentive toward further effort and does not guarantee positive results to the individual'.[24] That is, the capitalist society only accepts the desires that the market itself creates as incentive for entering the market war. The market is the criterion for the acceptable or non-acceptable desires. More than that, the market becomes the criterion for distinguishing the violence acceptable as beneficial, and therefore not seen as violence, but rather as competition or 'needed sacrifices', from the violence that must be violently combated. A possible example is the following affirmation of Fukuyama:

> The wars unleashed by these totalitarian ideologies were also of a new sort, involving the mass destruction of civilian populations and economic resources – hence the term, 'total war'. To defend themselves from this threat, liberal democracies were led to adopt military strategies like the bombing of Dresden or Hiroshima that in earlier ages would have been called genocidal.[25]

---

23 F. Hayek, *The Constitution of Liberty*, Chicago, University of Chicago Press, 1960, p. 42. The first italic is ours.
24 Hayek, *Constitution*, p. 43.
25 F. Fukuyama, *End of History*, p. 6.

Because they were carried out in the name of the market laws and liberal democracy, the historically corroborated genocides in Dresden and Hiroshima are not considered as such. Only violence engaged in by pre-capitalist and communist societies must be violently combated, because they are against the market laws. Violence by the market, and those acts carried out in its name are not seen as violence, because it is considered 'sacred' violence which clears society of the impure, pre-modern and 'communist' violence. When a violent action is defined as purifying, it is no longer seen as violence. Hence, genocide ceases to be genocide.

What generates this metamorphosis is the transcendentalization of the market and its endemic violence (competition) which come to be seen as a 'superior', a transcendental instance, which defines the criterion for distinguishing the pure from the impure in society. In Girardian terms, that means the sacred.

Coming back to the question of desire in Hayek, the lack of guaranteed positive results, or even more, the impossibility that all may achieve positive results, is a logical consequence of the structure of mimetic desire and of the dynamic of the modern economy itself. This means that there will always be unsatisfied people in the dynamic of mimetic desire. Hayek acknowledges this and states that capitalist society 'disregards the pain of unfulfilled desires aroused by the example of others. It appears cruel because it increases the desire of all in proportion as it increases its gifts to some. Yet so long as it remains a progressive society some must lead and the rest must follow.'[26]

Since progress is an unquestioned necessity in our societies and the efficiency in and of the market has become a dogma, it is easy to understand the conclusion of the 'inevitability' reached by Hayek and by many who defend the current neoliberal model of the capitalist economy. According to the logic of competition, of survival of the strongest, many – the weak – will be excluded from the market, sacrificed in their way. But, against those who defend the indelible dignity of all people and the consequent right to live, they say that those are the necessary sacrifices for progress. We cannot understand the strength of this affirmation if we do not keep in mind the theological sacrificial tradition that was so imposing in Western Christianity. Michael Novak, the prophet-theologian of the market, repossesses this tradition in defending the excluding logic of the market: 'If God so willed his beloved Son to suffer, why would He spare us?'[27]

---

26 Hayek, *Constitution*, p. 45

27 M. Novak, *The Spirit of Democratic Capitalism*, New York, Simon & Schuster, 1982, p. 341.

These ideas are a sample of how the disenchanting of the world, the secularizing and rationalizing of the world, did not mean the end of religion with its notion of transcendence, but rather the replacement of one type of myth with another. As Hinkelammert says,

> the secularizing of Christian mysteries did not change the fact of the existence of the mythical space. The social structures continue being projected in the infinite; and there are those who continue deriving from this projection in the infinite the norms and behaviour regarding such structures.[28]

In this same sense Hugo Assmann says that

> modernity secularizes and desacralizes things decentralizing and dispersing them (pluralism, sciences, subjectivity, individual liberties, self-interest, private initiative); and re-theologizes them in another level where one finds out what Marx called the 'perverse attitudes' (unrestricted market, self-accumulation of capital, scientism – idolatry of the market, idolatry of science).[29]

This transcendentalization of the market keeps in market relations a 'civility', which is grounded in violence (competition of all against all), and also keeps a certain 'harmony' in society in spite of all the violence waged against the 'incompetent ones'. It is a kind of civility that justifies all sacrifices of human lives as necessary claims of the market laws. This transcendentalization of the market's violence reminds us of René Girard's notion of religion.

For him, modern thinking did not manage to comprehend religion in its essence. Modern theories do not find a way to see the social function of the religious institution in spite of its presence for such a long time in human history. They only manage to see the reflection of its alienation or pathology. For Girard the religious is far from being a mere alienation or something useless because

> it humanizes violence; it protects man from his own violence by taking it out of his hands, transforming it into a transcendent and ever-present danger to be kept in check by the appropriate rites appropriately observed and by a modest and prudent demeanour.

---

28 F. Hinkelammert, *As armas ideológicas da morte*, S. Paulo, Paulinas, 1983, p. 279.

29 Hugo Assmann, 'Notas sobre of diálogo com cientistas e pesquisadores' in: Márcio Fabri dos Anjos (ed.), *Inculturação: desafios hoje*, Petrópolis-S. Paulo, Vozes-SOTER, 1994, pp. 139–56. Quoted on p. 141.

... To think religiously is to envision the city's destiny in terms of that violence whose mastery over man increases as man believes he has gained mastery over it. To think religiously (in the primitive sense) is to see violence as something superhuman, to be kept always at a distance and ultimately renounced.[30]

For this reason Girard says that no society can survive the spiral of uncontrolled reciprocal violence which follows the rivalries resulting from the mimetic structure of desire without religious mechanisms that transcendentalize violence and create a purifying violence which rescues society from the impure violence that can endanger its survival. In other words, the trancendentalized market provides to the exercised violence in the name of the market laws a purity that allows it to be perceived as something positive and creative. This transcendentalization of the market and the resulting sacrificialism have been criticized by several Liberation Theologians as a component of their critique of the idolatry of the market.[31]

In this sense we can say that the secularization of the modern world did not mean the end of religions, but the emergence of a new type of religion: the economic religion. This reasoning is in line with Girard's affirmation that 'there is no society without religion because without religion society cannot exist'.[32]

This way of conceiving the 'secularization' of Western society does not by itself answer the question of the contribution of theology in the formulation and implementation of an alternative project of society. The task of discerning the religions as well as the concrete notions of the sacred and transcendence and, in our case, the critique of the transcendence of the market and its sacrificial mechanisms could be done by other social theories or philosophies even without the participation of theology. Although it is very rare for us to see theoreticians from the areas of social sciences, economics or philosophy developing more frequent intuitions in a more systemic way and moving in this direction,[33] it is common for us to find terms such as 'fundamentalism', 'dogmatism', 'laissez-faire theology' and other theological expressions

---

30 Girard, *Violence and the Sacred*, pp. 134 and 135.

31 See, for instance, Assmann and Hinkelammert, *Idolatria do mercado*, 1989; Franz Hinkelammert, *Sacrificios humanos y sociedad occidental: Lucifer y la Bestia*, San José (Costa Rica), DEI, 1991; Hugo Assmann, *Crítica à lógica da exclusão*, São Paulo, Paulus, 1994; Jung Mo Sung, *Teologia e economia* and *Deus numa economia sem coração*, 2nd edn, São Paulo, Paulus, 1994.

32 Girard, *Violence and the Sacred*, p. 221.

33 Jung Mo Sung, 'Fundamentalismo econômico', *Estudos de Religião*, no 11 (Dec. 1995), São Bernardo do Campo, São Paulo, pp. 101–8.

in several authors who criticize neoliberalism and capitalist modernity. Boaventura Souza dos Santos, for instance, says that

> When the desirable was impossible it was left to God; when the desirable became possible it was left to science; today, when much of the possible is undesirable and some of the impossible is desirable we have to divide in half, to both God and science. . . . What distinguishes critical postmodern theory is the fact that for this theory radical needs are not deducible from a mere philosophical exercise no matter how radical it may be; they rather emerge from the social and aesthetic imagination, of which the concrete emancipating practices are capable. The re-enchanting of the world assumes the creative insertion of the utopian novelty of that which is closest to us.[34]

Actually, modernity believed that all the desirable was possible and it delivered to science and the market the implementation of these desires. Also in the name of this belief it demanded sacrifices of human lives. With this small correction, we fully agree that today we perceive much more clearly that 'much of the possible is undesirable and some of the impossible is desirable' and this raises again for us the problem of God.[35] Not a God who does not transcend the institutions and laws of the world, but a God who is beyond the world, who is neither identified with its injustices and sacrificial demands nor an object of certainty, but rather of hope. The recognition of the limits of human reason and action leads us not only to hope in God, but also to the difficult task of discerning between the several possible images of God at the basis of the social and aesthetical imagination that Santos talks about. And that is a theological task.

No doubt this theological task cannot be restricted to the critique of the images of God as the absolute, which are current in social thinking and ideologies. For, as we have briefly seen above, one of the pillars of neoliberal sacrificial discourse is the same Christian theology, or better said, a significant portion of it, which elaborated a theology of salvation centred in the concept of God's required necessary sacrifices. As Juan Luis Segundo used to say, we cannot produce a Theology of Liberation without first liberating theology, namely, without a self-criticism of Christianity's theological tradition and even its history.

---

34 Boaventura Souza Santos, *Pela mão de Alice: o social e o político na pós-modernidade*, São Paulo, Cortez, 1995, p. 106.

35 On the important question of the historical feasibility of transcendental concepts and hopes from the standpoint of his critique, see: Franz Hinkelammert, *Crítica da razão utópica*, São Paulo, Paulinas, 1985.

I know that there are several other questions that may and must be dealt with in this debate, but I have no illusion of exhausting the subject. Thus, let us return to the problem of social exclusion and growing insensitivity about it.

Structural unemployment and exclusion

This chapter's central objective is not to analyse the reality and logic of exclusion, but rather to debate the role of theology and its contribution to the subject. Therefore, the following more concrete analysis regarding the problem does not have an exhaustive character, but is instrumental in the pursuit of our main objective.

A first point we should make clear is that social exclusion is not exclusive to Third World countries. If we take, as an example, the American continent, at first sight we perceive two well distinct blocs: North America (USA and Canada) and Latin America. In both we will find some similar situations. The more salient is the great concentration of wealth[36] and the contrast between pockets of wealth amidst a sea of poverty (in Latin America) and pockets of poverty amidst a sea of wealth (in North America).

The new fact of this social contrast, which in one form or another always existed on our continent, is the segregation that takes place between these two social groups. Previously there existed channels of communication between the rich and poor sectors of the population, both in geographical and economic terms. Today the alienation becomes visible on the walls of closed residential condominiums, clubs, private locations and other mechanisms; and, in a general way it becomes less visible, due to the disappearance or shrinking of the economic relations between these two sectors.

An increasing number of people in the United States and the majority in Latin America are being excluded from the market, and, therefore, from the gains of development, from the conditions of a dignified life, and even worse, from the possibility of survival. To be excluded from the market does not mean, however, to be excluded from society and from the reach of the means of social communication that socialize the same consumption desires. Thus we have a tragic situation where the poor (young and adult) are stimulated to desire the consumption of sophisticated and superfluous goods while being denied the possi-

---

36 Wealth became so concentrated that 358 billionaires in the whole world control properties which are superior to the total income of countries including 45% of the world population.

bility of access to the satisfaction of their basic needs for a dignified survival.

One of the fundamental causes of this process of exclusion is, no doubt, the structural unemployment that affects the continent and almost the whole world. The current unemployment is called structural because this is not a circumstantial situation, caused by an economic recession that would phase out or soften out with economic growth. The opposite is true, as businesses increase their profits and see their stocks going up in the stock market precisely for dismissing their employees. The countries of the OECD – Organization for Economic Cooperation and Development – already have almost 40 million unemployed.

This structural unemployment is one of the consequences of the current model of the globalization of the economy, the technological revolution and the increasing financial nature of the wealth. These factors are generating such a world economy that, according to Peter Drucker, 'in the industrial economy the production ceased to be "connected" to jobs; and the movements of capital, not trade (whether of goods or service) became the moving forces of the world economy.'[37]

This situation can be seen as the crowning of a process of inversion as described by Max Weber in his famous book *The Protestant Ethic and the Spirit of Capitalism*: in capitalism,

> Man is dominated by the making of money, by acquisition as the ultimate purpose of his life. Economic acquisition is no longer subordinated to man as the means for the satisfaction of his material needs. This reversal of what we should call the natural relationship, so irrational from a naive point of view, is evidently a leading principle of capitalism as it is foreign to all peoples not under capitalistic influence.[38]

In premodern societies people worked to live. In capitalist societies people began to live to accumulate wealth. Now, with the globalization of the economy, technology and the new forms of management which increased productivity, job reduction programmes generate more profits for business and growing income for investors and managers. Even more, the financial system which should be linked to, and at the service of, the production system, became bigger, more important,

---

37 Peter Drucker, 'The changes in the world economy', *Política Externa*, vol. 1, no 3 (Dec. 1992), São Paulo, Paz e Terra, p. 17 (original in English, 1986). This author is considered the 'gurus' guru' of business administration.
38 Max Weber, *The Protestant Ethic and the Spirit of Capitalism*, New York, Charles Scribner's, 1958, p. 53.

and to a great extent disconnected from the production. The wealth is increasingly financial and, to a large extent has become 'fictional'. Today it is not basically made any more of tangible goods, but of blinking numbers in computer monitors. The problem is that any critique of this logic as irrational is labelled by the same Weber, who criticized so much the introduction of values in science, as 'a naive point of view'.

Michel Albert, an important French businessman and president of the Paris based CEPII – Centre of Prospective Studies and International Information – criticizing the current capitalist model wrote: 'Profit for what? Never raise this question because you will be immediately expelled from the sanctuary for raising doubt about the first article of the credo: *the purpose of profit is profit*. On this, no compromise.'[39]

The problem is that this desire, this limitless pursuit of wealth for the sake of wealth, produces two very grave, unintentional side-effects. The first is the threat to the ecological system. The voracity for more profits ends up by destroying the ecological system that took billions of years to be formed and makes our human life possible. Furthermore it also produces the grave social crisis that we see in our countries. The crisis is not about poverty and social contrasts only, but also about unrestrained violence and the growing traffic and consumption of drugs. This is a situation which reminds us of the myth of King Midas who died of hunger surrounded by mountains of gold. For, as Aristotle used to say, coveting the accumulation of wealth under the illusion that money can buy infinite means of living ends up by destroying precisely the 'good life', namely, 'life in community'.[40] For life can only be maintained and reproduced inside the concrete limits of the community and environment.

We should further add two important data to help us understand better the precariousness of the Latin American reality. The first is the fact that there is a great deal of difference between being poor and unemployed in rich countries, with social programmes that really work, and being in this situation in countries that are drastically eliminating the few and inefficient remaining social programmes, in the name of the neoliberally inspired economic adjustment.

The second is the fact that in almost all countries in Latin America we find what we may call the 'distinct juxtaposed times and spaces'. Inside the same country there are social groups that live in distinct

---

39 Michel Albert, *Capitalismo vs. capitalismo*, São Paulo, Fundação Fides-Loyola, 1992, p. 239. [English language edn: *Capitalism against Capitalism*, trans. Paul Haviland, Indianapolis, John Wiley & Son, 1992.]

40 See Ulrich Duchrow, *Alternatives to Global Capitalism*, Utrecht, International Books, 1995, p. 51.

historical times. Some still live in a premodern culture, utilizing production techniques of the time of the agricultural revolution, with no
access to the kind of formal education available in industrialized urban
societies. Others belong to the second technological revolution, the
Fordist industrial era, and still a third group who live in a postmodern
culture, with access to the state-of-the-art technologies. This disconnection of time indicates a grave economic problem. Many desire to
work, but are not prepared for the few vacancies in businesses that
have been modernized under the pressure of the market.

Alongside this disconnection we have the grave problem of 'spacial-
cultural distancing'. The elite of our countries feel more identified with
the elites of the rich countries than with the majority of our poor population. In a certain way we could say that our elites and the middle
classes feel themselves as belonging to the community of consumers of
the world market rather than belonging to our nations, to our national
societies.[41] In such a situation it is much more difficult to get the adherence of the middle and upper classes to policies aiming at a solution of
the social problems in our countries.

Culture of insensitivity

A society based on a logic of exclusion generates and, at the same
time, feeds on a culture of insensitivity. Unfortunately we can witness in our daily life the growth of insensitivity regarding the suffering others, especially the poor. Not even the frequent murdering of
children who live in the streets shock our societies any more. After all,
they are poor.

This culture of insensitivity, which borders on cynicism, did not grow
by chance. It springs out from several historical and social factors,
besides other anthropological ones. For lack of space we will quote
only some factors of major concern for us.

There exists in our society an idea of the inevitability of inequality
and social exclusion. This thesis received a major boost with the fall
of the communist bloc. With the failure of the alternative model, the
thesis that capitalism, with its neoliberal ideology, represented the 'end
of history'[42] got a previously unimaginable support. With the spreading of the thesis that there is no possible alternative, the current social
situation came to be seen as inevitable.

---

41 About this, see, for instance: Renato Ortiz, *Mundialização e cultura*, 2nd
edn, São Paulo, Brasiliense, 1994.
42 F. Fukuyama, *The End of History*.

Not only inevitable but also just. We witness the growth of what Galbraith called the 'culture of contentment': the notion that those well integrated in the market 'are just receiving what they fairly deserve' and that, therefore, 'whether the good fortune is deserved or a reward for personal merit, there is no plausible justification for any action which could harm or inhibit it – to reduce that which is or might be enjoyed'.[43] The other side of the coin is that the poor are seen as guilty for their poverty and are getting their just reward. Thus, the current concentrating and excluding mechanisms of the market are seen as 'incarnations' of a judge from a transcendental justice. This is a secularized version of the theology of retribution, 'a doctrine that is cozy and tranquilizing for those who possess many goods in this world while producing resignation and a sense of guilt in those who do not get the goods,'[44] and which was so criticized by Jesus and by the reformers with the theology of grace. For the more ecclesiastical environments there is the modern religious version of the theology of prosperity.

Social inequality came to be seen by the majority not only as inevitable and just, but also as beneficient.[45] Here we have the proof of how neoliberalism managed to become the hegemonic ideology of our time. For neoliberals, who have an unshakable faith in the capacity of the 'invisible hand'[46] of the market to solve economic and social problems, the deepening of the social inequality and exclusion is a good sign. Inequality for them is both the mover of economic progress, because it encourages competition among people, and the result of a society based on competition. Furthermore the social crisis, which is always seen as a passing phase, would be for them the sign that the economy is following the good road of deregulation and with no more intervention by the state in the economy for social purpose.

---

43 John Kenneth Galbraith, *A cultura do contentamento*, São Paulo, Pioneira, 1992, p. 12. [English language edn: *The Culture of Contentment*, Wilmington, Mass., Houghton Mifflin, 1993.]

44 Gustavo Gutiérrez, *Falar de Deus a partir do sofrimento do inocente: uma reflexão sobre o livro de Jó*, Petrópolis, Vozes, 1987, p. 53. [English language edn: *On Job: God-Talk and the Suffering of the Innocent*, Maryknoll, NY, Orbis Books, 1990.]

45 See, for instance, Suzanne de Brunhoff, *A hora do mercado. Crítica do liberalismo*, São Paulo, Ed. Unesp, 1991; Perry Anderson, 'El despliegue del neoliberalismo y sus lecciones para la isquierda', *Pasos*, San José (Costa Rica), DEI, no 66, July–August 1996, pp. 23–30.

46 Adam Smith's concept of 'invisible hand' comes from the theological concept of the divine providence, that by its turn, may be interpreted in terms of the theology of retribution. I believe it would be worthwhile to explore, in depth, the meaning and social implications of these links.

Based on the equivocation of identifying economic growth with human and social development, the current conductors of the economic and cultural process propose the modernization of the economy and the whole society as the only way to go. Modernizing is understood as the funnelling of all the debates and actions from the economic and political areas into the field of instrumental reason. That means the elimination from the debate of all human and social values, all duties and rights of people and nations which preceded (in logical and chronological order) the market system, and to reduce everything to the issue of efficiency in the relation between scarce means and the economic goal of limitless accumulation of wealth.[47]

On this point the former finance minister of Brazil and ardent defender of neoliberalism, Roberto Campos, states that modernization, the only viable way for Latin America, 'presupposes a *cruel mystique* of the effort and the cult of efficiency'.[48]

'Cruel mystique' is an expression difficult to understand for those who do not share this neoliberal outlook. How can a mystique be cruel? And how can a cruel mystique be something good? A mystique, as Leonardo Boff says, is the 'secret mover of all commitment, that enthusiasm that permanently animates the militant'.[49] It is the force that helps us not only to do good, but also to overcome the temptations of sin. And what is sin for neoliberals?

For them the fundamental and originating cause of economic and social evils, namely, original sin, in religious terms, is the 'pretence of knowledge'[50] of the economists in relation to the market, the basis of all state interventions and social movements. According to Hayek and his followers one's impossibility of perfect awareness of all the factors and relations involved in the market results in the impossibility of one's knowingly and intentionally pursuing the solution of economic and social problems. In other words, we human beings should abandon the desire of building a better society. For whenever we come up with an intention to do good we end up by intervening in the market with state

---

47 On the irrationality of this contemporary reason, see F. Hinkelammert, *El mapa del emperador*, San José (Costa Rica), DEI, 1996.

48 Roberto Campos, *Alem do cotidiano*, Rio de Janeiro, Record, 2nd edn, 1985.

49 Leonardo Boff, 'Alimentar a nossa mística', *Cadernos Fé e Política*, no 9, Petrópolis, 1993, pp. 7–25, quoted on p. 19.

50 Friedrich A. von Hayek, 'The Pretence of Knowledge', in Assar Lindbeck (ed.), *Nobel Lectures – Economic Sciences, 1969–1980*, Singapore, London, New Jersey, The Nobel Foundation, 1992, pp. 179–88. This lecture was presented by Hayek at the occasion of his receiving the Nobel Prize in Economics, in 1974.

or civil actions aiming at reducing unemployment and social inequality. According to their dogmas any intervention in the market results in reduction of efficiency and consequently in economic and social crisis.

The only way open to us, according to them, is to have faith in the always, and necessarily beneficial invisible hand of the market and see the suffering of the unemployed and excluded as 'necessary sacrifices' demanded by the market laws. Thus, this mystique which should help us to overcome the 'temptation to do good',[51] appears to be cruel. This cruel mystique is the secret mover of neoliberal commitment and thus expresses itself in the cult of efficiency in the market and of the market, but not in the service of the God of mercy and life.

The good news of a God who is love

In the face of a world that lives out the idolatry of the market, that looks for justice and salvation in the fulfilment of the market laws, what should be the mission of the Christian churches? What should be the good news that we must announce to the world to keep us faithful to the gospel? What are the contributions that theology and churches should bring to the process of formulation and construction of alternative models? Some ideas have been already developed in the course of this chapter. Now, more for the purpose of provoking and stimulating discussion on the subject rather than bringing it to a close, we want to present some others.

Thus, first of all, and to avoid any misunderstanding, it must be clarified that the critique of the idolatry of the market does not mean a critique of the market as such, but only of its sacralization, namely of the absolutizing of its laws. One must be careful lest the critique of the sacralization of the market laws take us to the extreme of the same logic, which is its demonizing. It is not possible, especially in complex societies, to organize the economy without mercantile relations. As Hugo Assmann says, 'among other undeniable things, in the field of human interactions in complex societies, is the functionality of partially self-regulating systems regarding human behaviours. In economics this question has a name . . .: the market'.[52]

---

51 This is the title of a novel by O. Drucker, *The Temptation to Do Good*. See footnote 18 in Chapter 1.

52 H. Assmann, 'Mercado mundializado e crise do sujeito', in *Metáforas novas para reencantar a educação*, Piracicaba, Unimep, 1996, pp. 63–84. Quoted on p. 64.

With that in mind, let's return to the problem of sin and idolatry. We need, in our theologies and pastoral practices, to unmask the spirit of idol worship – the human and social work of action and interrelation risen to the category of the Divine – which demands continual sacrifices of human lives in the name of accumulation of wealth and limitless consumption. We need to show that the root of all economic and social evils is not our struggle to live in a more human and just society but rather, as the Apostle Paul teaches us: 'the root of all evils is the love of money' (1 Tim. 6.10).

Idolatry as a theological concept is also utilized by theorists such as Fromm and Horkheimer to account for this apparently contradictory phenomenon in the modern world: devotion, promises and human sacrifices in a world that apparently calls itself secularized. But because it is a concept coming from the biblical tradition and theology, sociologists and economists feel some difficulty in the use of this concept. For the concept of idolatry can also presuppose the existence of a true God or at least a real or conceptual transcendence beyond all human limits. Yet this concept has the advantage of showing the process of absolutizing (sacralizing) a human institution that demands human sacrifices in exchange for redeeming promises.

The concept of sacralization of society, which was demonstrated by Durkheim in the totemic system and which could be very well utilized to analyse so-called 'economic fundamentalism' or 'neoliberal dogma' has, on the one hand, the advantage of not presupposing a true deity or transcendence, and on the other hand, the disadvantage of not calling for the notion of sacrifices of human lives. In my opinion, the concept of idolatry presupposes that of the sacralization of a social system and goes further, explaining the sacrificial logic underlying the sacralization process of human works and institutions. This logic, as we have seen, has the capacity to reverse the notion of good and evil. In this sense the critique of the idolatry of the market is a fundamental contribution of theology to the current debate about neoliberalism.

In the face of this we should re-establish a simple and irrefutable truth: the economy must exist for the life of all people rather than people existing for economic laws based in the objective of accumulation of wealth. In other words, we must explain the difference between an economy turned to the accumulation of wealth and an economy organized for the overcoming of poverty and making possible a dignified life for the whole population. This is one of the most important ways to translate in today's language the teaching of Jesus: 'The sabbath was made for humankind, and not humankind for the sabbath' (Mark 2.27).

The poor people of America, the excluded ones from our societies, do not hunger just for bread but also, and intensely so, for their denied humanity, and for God. They hunger for a God who does not exclude anyone (see Acts 10.35 and Rom. 2.11) and who is among human beings 'that they may have life, and have it abundantly' (John 10.10). So that this good news be able to yield fruits in our society we must confront one of that society's fundamental problems, which is a basic theological task for the churches: the critique of the theology of retribution, in the version of the 'culture of contentment' and of the theology of prosperity. For they sacralize the injustice of the world, revealing a god (idol) that legitimizes the culture of insensitivity while blaming the victims of exclusion in our society. To that one must counterpoise the theology of grace. One must show that God is neither behind the sufferings and injustices, nor the provider of the wealth of the minorities, and announce as well that one cannot take the name of God in vain to justify injustices and cynicisms, since God does not save us because of merits but because of grace. And if we want to live according to the grace of the Lord, we need to recognize, in a gratuitous way, beyond the market law, the right of all people to have the possibility of a good and dignified life. In other words, we must recover the value of solidarity and equality.

In sociological terms we are talking about a society that includes everyone; a world that includes many worlds, where different people, Jews and gentiles, learn to respect differences and equal right to a dignified and joyous life for all. No doubt, such a society will be one in which the market is an important component of the economy. But certainly it will be neither a sacralized nor an omnipotent market. There will also be government and social democratic mechanisms of control and complementation of market mechanisms so as to ensure that the basic rights of all people will be respected and the ecological system preserved.

This attitude of an accepting criticism that sees the market positively but refuses to give up solidarity objectives entails, as Hugo Assmann says, 'a new reflection about the very conception of the individual and collective ethical agent'. 'It has to do with thinking not only about individual ethical options but also about the material and institutional objectivation of values under the form of normalization of the human conviviality with strong self-regulating connotations.'[53] It is the challenge of conceiving ethical decisions correlated with the partially self-regulating mechanisms of the market. This position con-

---

53 Assmann, 'Mercado mundializado', p. 64.

flicts not only with liberal and neoliberal thinking which attributes to the market the capacity to generate the good unintentionally, as a kind of inborn solidarity, but also with sectors that still attribute to the state a messianic character and as such favour a concentration of decision in its hands.

To struggle for a society that includes everyone does not mean to have an a priori political project, but rather to make of this maxim a criterion of discernment among several global or possible partial projects. In more immediate terms it means to struggle for the creation of more jobs and other income generating economic mechanisms for the excluded sectors of society. This means two battlefronts.

The first battlefront is the policy of reform of the state to make it recover not only the political will to solve social problems but also the economic capacity for social programmes as well as for intervening in, and providing direction to, the economy. In this political struggle we should not forget the fundamental task of strengthening civil society. It must be a counterpoint to the state, resisting its bureaucratic and self-corrupting tendencies, as well as the tendency of subservience to the ruling elites.

The second battlefront is in enabling workers to adapt to the new techniques of production, or to create new types of economic activities, as, for instance, co-operatives or social entities. Such enabling should be implemented through the public system of formal education, a point that leads us back to the problem of the state, and through processes of popular or 'para-formal' education.

However, for this struggle to achieve the adherence and support of the great majority of the population we need to create or strengthen spiritualities of solidarity that counteract the cruel mystique of neoliberalism. We need a spirituality able to make people desire – not the desire of the capitalist elite, of imitating the consumer patterns of the First World elites and the limitless accumulation of goods, but rather the desire of Jesus 'that they may have life, and have it abundantly' (John 10.10), without confusing the quality of life with the quantity of consumption.

Without such spirituality we will not be able to deal with a basic challenge, that is, 'to establish priorities for political action related to a new conception of development, accessible to all people and capable of maintaining the ecological balance'.[54] We must change the objective that guides the economy, so that it will stop being the imitation

---

54 Celso Furtado, *Brasil, a construção interrompida*, 2nd edn, Rio de Janeiro, Paz e Terra, 1992, pp. 76–7.

of consumption patterns of the First World elites (which present themselves as a model for humankind). For without this change it will not be possible to end the economic segregation found in Latin American countries. In theological terms, this change of desire is conversion. A new spirituality that changes the desires by changing the desire's model is a profoundly theological subject.

No doubt the spreading of this spirituality is a challenge to society and also – indeed a very serious one – to our churches and to all Christians. For the 'world's evil', the exclusion which is found in the world, is also found in our midst, as we find ourselves in the midst of the world. Thus, even if we pray to God to 'protect them from the evil one' (John 17.15) often we are more a witness of an idol that discriminates and excludes than of a God who in grace and mercy loves and welcomes all without distinction.

In conclusion I would like to recall another very important point. In a globalized world the solutions for problems cannot be thought of in local and national terms alone. One needs international articulation and co-ordination. And here the Christian churches can be of great service to humankind. The Christian churches and the international ecumenical organizations are some of the few institutions that not only possess both local and international networks but also are concerned about the life of the poor and the excluded ones in our continent. We must make the best possible use of these infrastructures and connections as well as of the body of knowledge of the diverse currents and traditions so that life, 'the Spirit's wind', that dwells in all human beings, the great God's gift, be honoured in its dignity and integrity.

These few and insufficient clues were offered not to exhaust the subject matter, but to help us not forget that we must incarnate the good news of Jesus in today's historical conditions. Theologians and churches must assume this task of thinking and practising in a creative way so that our faith can make a relevant contribution to the cause of the excluded.

4

Economics and Religion: Challenges for Christianity in the Twenty-first Century

The theme of 'evangelization and the Third Millennium' is the order of the day. For us to be able to announce the good news to the poor and to the whole of humankind we need to know the main problem that afflicts them. When the time-line is the third millennium, it is almost impossible for one to come up with analysis of problems and their causes. On the other hand, we cannot reduce the time-line only to the immediate and everyday life of small groups, especially when we are living through the globalization process.

That being the case, I want to sketch here an analysis that has as its time horizon not the millennium but the turn of the century to try to understand what are today's great changes and challenges that will determine the coming decades, and how the capitalist system is reacting to such changes. In this way I am going to privilege, as I have done in other chapters, the relation between theology and economics. Not only because as a Liberation Theologian I believe it to be of fundamental importance to deal with the relation between the announcing of the good news to the poor and the economic structures, but also because the economy, a part of the social life that is becoming almost omnipresent in today's world, is being more and more related with theology and religion by the economists and social scientists themselves.

A global vision of changes

Whoever minimally follows the discussions and analysis about our time is already acquainted with the idea that we are living not only in an era of great changes but also in a change of era. Let's see some major components of this process.

First, with the end of the communist bloc almost one third of the world population is having to learn, with great difficulty, to go from a centralized economy where all or at least the major decisions were

76

carried out by the state, to a market economy, with its risks, possibility of enrichment and social inequalities. The social and economic crisis and the ethnic conflicts in the European East are visible signs of the difficulties of this process. In this context China is a special case. Not only for its population of 1.2 billion inhabitants, but also for its model of changes which has produced a yearly rate of economic growth above 10 per cent in the last 15 years. A progressively greater economic integration in globalization, quite apart from the maintenance of its political model, is going to change profoundly the economic configuration of the planet.

Second, the globalization of the economy, made possible by various technological transformations, is retiring the notion of national economy and perceptibly shrinking the power and influence of the national state. Alongside the possibility of production and consumption without the limitations of national barriers it is important to highlight the huge size of the current financial market (around 15 trillion dollars) and its highly speculative character, since only 15 per cent of this total is linked to the productive system. In this time of virtual reality, we can say that a good portion of international capitalism turns around a virtual wealth.

Third, this process of globalization of the economy has been accompanied by another, namely, globalization of culture. The concept of global economy has to do with one single structure underlying any and all economies whose dynamics can be measured by the economists, with indicators such as international exchange and investments. However, in the cultural sphere, to be worldwide is not the same as to be uniform. The worldwide culture connects itself with the movement of globalization of societies, but that has to do with a specific symbolic universe of the current civilization, with a vision of world. 'In this sense, it goes along with other world visions, setting up among them hierarchies, conflicts and accommodations.'[1] It does not imply the elimination of other local cultural manifestations but a process where it feeds on them. An example of this is language. English is a worldwide language. In some cases English predominates (as in technology, international business and in the Internet), but in other moments and other spheres it will either be absent or have little weight (family and religion). 'Its transversal character reveals and expresses the globalization of the modern life; its worldwide character preserves other languages in the interior of this transglossic space.'[2]

---

1 Renato Ortiz, *Mundialização e cultura*, 2nd edn, São Paulo, Brasilliense, 1994, p. 29.
2 Ortiz, *Mundialização*, p. 29.

If in the beginnings of capitalism and of the cultural modernization in the West, work ethics and work culture prevailed, in the current worldwide culture, consumption enjoys a distinctive position, and has become one of the major world definers of legitimacy of behaviours and values.

Fourth, technological change, also known as technological revolution, is creating an era dominated by industries based on the intellectual capacity of the human being. Differently from the previous pattern, where the majority of industries had their geographical spaces determined by the localization of natural resources, the ownership of capital and the type of needed manpower, these new industries do not have predetermined places and can establish themselves wherever is more convenient to them.

Fifth, the end of the communist bloc and the resulting exclusive dominance of capitalism did not mean the maintenance of a dominant centre of economic or political power. In the nineteenth century the rules of international trade were formulated and imposed by England, and after World War Two, by the United States. But in the twenty-first century the globalized economy will no longer have a 'strong' centre, but rather several 'loose' centres scattered in big transnational corporations, in some countries such as the United States, Japan, Germany and in multilateral organizations such as the World Bank and the World Trade Organization. A problem to be considered at this point is how can a globalized economic system operate effectively under the command of several loose centres?

Sixth, besides these questions we still have the demographic problem. The population of the poor countries continues to grow, while that of the rich countries stabilizes itself. 'While the industrial democracies accounted for more than one-fifth of the earth's population in 1950, that share had dropped to one-sixth by 1985, and is forecast to shrivel to less than one-tenth by 2025'.[3] Added to this we also have the ever more brutal concentration of wealth in the hands of a minority. These factors generate the phenomenon of economic migrants striving for survival or better days, not to mention political refugees. In the eighteenth century Europe went through a similar demographic problem and the discovered solution was emigration to the New World. However, today the rich countries shut their doors to immigrants, to the 'new barbarians',[4] because with the new technological revolution

---

3 Paul Kennedy, *Preparing for the Twenty-First Century*, New York, Random House, 1993, p. 45.

4 Jean Cristophe Rufin, *O império e os novos bárbaros*, 2nd edn, Rio de Janeiro, Record, 1992.

unskilled manpower is not needed and the industrialized countries, especially in Europe, also have the problem of structural unemployment. Beside this migration problem, we also have that of an ageing population, which is a serious problem for the social security systems, to the extent that a proportionally smaller number of contributors will have to support an ever-growing number of retirees.

Seventh, I want to refer to one more factor in the process of the great transformation we are going through today: the ecological question. Certainly the environmental problem has been the motivation of more debates than concrete actions, at the economic and political levels. In this sense, it should not be part of the list of factors which today are changing the configuration of the world. On the other hand, the growth of ecological consciousness, or at least the consciousness about environmental problems and its influence, in the debate regarding the new theoretical paradigms, allow us to bring it to the fore. From the ecological standpoint, the high consumption patterns of the elites in rich countries, as well as the ones in countries that imitate the consumption pattern of the latter, the excessive demands and the squandering habits of the populations integrated in the world market, plus the billions of excluded people in poor or developing countries, who also aspire to increase their consumption levels (taking as model of imitation of desire the consumption patterns of the middle class and the elites[5]), constitute a serious attack on our planet. Environmentalists thus consider this question as a race against time.

In this sense, Cristovam Buarque says that

the crisis of modernity will not be solved with an advance in modernity. A different modernity is called for regarding not only means but also purposes and types of society. It is no longer possible or desirable to reach the levels of wealth of the 'rich countries'. There is no longer socialism to be copied. The modernization of the economy and the distribution of its results are not enough. It is necessary to modernize the modernization.[6]

This point of view, that criticizes the myth of progress and economic development and contests the assumption that development for its own sake is desirable and therefore that economic production is the most useful measure of the material success of a country, has pro-

---

5 The problem of imitation of consumption desire was dealt with in Chapters 2 and 3.

6 Cristovam Buarque, *A revolução na esquerda e a invenção do Brasil*, Rio de Janeiro, Paz e Terra, 1992, p. 24.

voked counter-attacks from many economists. For the optimists the natural resources do not constitute an absolute quantity which is being constantly consumed; on the contrary, for them many resources are created by human inventiveness and work, and technology has an infinite capacity of producing new resources.

New time, new ideology?

For a more complete vision of our great scenario we also need a look at the ideology that is dynamizing and bringing consistency to this process.

Until recently this relation between technologies and institutions on one hand and beliefs and ideologies on the other was not appreciated in social analysis. This was so because most social scientists, both the theoreticians under the influence of Marxism and the neoclassic liberals, shared the same vision of the world: the world as a machine. They believed, and many still do, that the world and society are like a very complicated machine whose functioning may be understood if we carefully and meticulously gather the parts that compose it. From this premise they concluded that the behaviour of the system, as a whole, could be deduced from a simple summing up of those components, whether individuals or social classes. A lever pulled in a certain part of the machine, with a certain amount of strength, would produce regular and predictable results in another part of the machine. It is based on these premises that the IMF and the World Bank impose their economic adjustments in an 'impersonal' and 'universal' way, that is, as valid for all societies. Similarly, starting from these premises, many people of good will participated in the social, political and ecclesial movements with the unshakeable certainty of the inevitability of the success of the construction of the Kingdom of Freedom or the Kingdom of God.

In neoclassical economic theory the 'scientific' basis of neoliberalism, the basic part of the machine, is the rational man. This means that society is seen as constituted of individuals who act in line with the rational estimation of their interests, an estimation that envisages maximization of benefits and minimization of costs. Besides reducing the human being to an essentially egotistical being, the analogy of the world as a well-oiled machine led economists to think that the world is fundamentally balanced and harmonic. 'Once started the machine glides along, each component part contributing to its serene progress.'[7]

---

7 Paul Ormerod, *The Death of Economics*, New York, St. Martin's Press, 1994, p. 41.

From then on, economic growth is seen as running peacefully provided that there is no undue intervention by government and labour unions. The problems of economic fluctuations and unemployment simply disappeared from today's hegemonic economic theory.

Faith in this conception of the world is so strong that the University of Chicago, the great centre of neoclassical thinking, had five of its professors winning the Nobel Prize in Economics from 1990 to 1995. And two of the more renowned neoclassical economists of our times, also Nobel Prize winners, Gary Becker and James Buchanan, built up their academic careers applying the neoclassic economic methodology to non-economic phenomena such as politics, bureaucracy, racism, family and fertility. In the case of birth control, for instance, there are economists from this current sponsoring the idea that the best way to control natality is to show to the parents that investment in producing babies does not compensate in the face of the small and uncertain return they would receive in the form of caring in their old age. Rather than having children they should invest in private retirement funds!

For this type of thinking, the increase of social exclusion and other social problems are not, in truth, problems at all, but rather signs that we are heading toward a real and definitive solution. They are signs that the government is abandoning its undue intention of intervening in the market in the name of social goals, and is allowing the free running of the market. In the end, what we call social problems are only problems of groups of inefficient individuals who deservedly were left out by the market's system of competition.

This mechanistic and individualistic vision of the world was expressed in a clear and beautiful way in Margaret Thatcher's famous declaration that what they call society is something that does not exist and that what exist are the individuals that constitute it.

Today, more and more scientists come to the conclusion that this way of seeing the natural and social world as a machine is not the most appropriate one. Instead of machine they are using the analogy of a living organism. Behaviours of the system are not deducible from the sum of individual behaviours; they are too complex to be represented by a mechanistic approach. With that they are renouncing claims to absolute certainty in diagnosis and the possibility of 'scientific' foresight.[8]

----

8 This is a very important and broad theme, but an extrapolation in this book. For an introductory vision we recommend the book by Edgar Morin, *Introdução ao pensamento complexo*, Lisbon, Piaget, 1991. As applied to the field of education and the debate regarding the market, see the excellent book by Hugo Assmann, *Metáforas novas para reencantar a educação*, Piracicaba,

Furthermore, this new way of seeing the world and human society brings to the economic debate the problem of ideology and of individual and social values. The economic dynamic is not seen any longer simply as the result of the interaction of quantifiable factors, a fundamental principle of the economic sciences since the end of the nineteenth century. It is also seen as the result of interactions with values and other non-quantifiable factors.

In this sense, Lester Thurow, professor of economics at the famous MIT, wrote that 'societies flourish when beliefs and technologies are congruent; decline when the inevitable changes in beliefs and technologies become incongruent'.[9] This is not a new idea, but stated by a famous economist in the United States is a sign of the times. For him the demise of feudalism did not happen only due to the technological revolution and new institutions, especially regarding property and trade. Alongside,

> capitalism also needed changes in its ideology. In the Middle Ages avarice was the worst of all sins and the merchant could never be pleasing to God. Capitalism needed a world where avarice was a virtue and the merchant could be most pleasing to God. The individual needed to believe that he or she had not just the right, but the duty to make as much moneys as possible. The idea that maximizing personal consumption is central to individual welfare is less than two hundred years old. Without this belief the incentive structure of capitalism has no meaning and economic growth has no purpose.[10]

If in its beginning capitalism needed this linkage of the belief with religion, once victorious it could give up this shelter, at least at the level of explicit speech. About this Weber said: 'In the field of its highest development, in the United States, the pursuit of wealth, stripped of its ethical-religious meaning, tends to become associated with purely mundane passions.'[11]

Capitalism no longer needs religion to legitimate itself, and has got rid of its archenemy, communism. Thus, it is natural that many agree

---

Unimep, 1996. As applied to the debate of the economic sciences, see the book of Paul Ormerod, *The Death of Economics*.

9 Lester Thurow, *The Future of Capitalism*, New York, William Morrow and Company, 1969, p. 12.

10 Thurow, *Future of Capitalism*, p. 11. The classic work on the subject continues to be Max Weber's *The Protestant Ethic and the Spirit of Capitalism*, New York, Charles Scribner's Sons, 1958.

11 Weber, *Protestant Ethic*, p. 182.

with the thesis that history has come to an end.[12] As Thurow says, 'capitalism and democracy now live in a unique period where effectively they have no viable competitors for the allegiance of the minds of their citizens. It has been called "the end of history".'[13] However, if it is true that there is a relation between technology and institutions of a given society and ideology,[14] what are the implications of the big changes (as we previously saw) for the composition of current capitalism? In other words, will these big changes demand, or are they already demanding, changes in the ideological field (the alternative being inefficiency of the market system)? That is not due only to technological changes, but also to the end of the communist bloc which made the problem of its own internal contradictions – up until then left on the back burner in the face of external confrontations – inescapable to the capitalist world.

With this we do not mean that neoliberalism,[15] the hegemonic ideology of our time, is in crisis especially in its final phase. As Perry Anderson says,

> the neoliberal project continues exhibiting an impressive vitality. . . . The political agenda continues to be dictated by neoliberal parameters even when its moment of economic performance seems austere and disastrous. How to explain this second life in the advanced capitalist world? One fundamental reason was clearly the victory of neoliberalism in other parts of the world, namely, the fall of communism in Eastern Europe and in the Soviet Union . . . There are no neoliberals more intransigent in the world than the 'reformers' of the East.[16]

However, there are signs that something new is happening in this field. Recently George Soros, a stockbroker tycoon who manages a 16 billion dollar investment fund, and a professed disciple of Karl Popper,

---

12 F. Fukuyama, *The End of History and the Last Man*, New York, The Free Press, 1992.

13 Thurow, *Future of Capitalism*, p. 64.

14 For a systematic vision of this relation, see, for instance, F. Hinkelammert, *Democracia y totalitarianismo*, San José, DEI, 1987, p. 12–44.

15 On neoliberalism, see, for instance, Emir Sader (ed.), *Pós-neoliberalismo*, São Paulo, Paz e terra, 1955. A teological vision with the analysis of the problem of the idolatry see, for instance, Jung Mo Sung, *Deus numa economia sem coração*, 2nd edn, São Paulo, Paulus, 1994, and Hugo Assmann, *Crítica à lógica da exclusão*, São Paulo: Paulus, 1995.

16 Perry Anderson, 'El despliegue del neoliberalismo y sus lecciones para la izquierda', *Pasos*, San José (Costa Rica), DEI, no 66, Jul–Aug. 1996, pp. 23–30. Quoted on p. 26.

wrote a long article, 'The Capitalist Threat', attacking fiercely the current capitalist system:

> Although I have made a fortune in the money market, I fear now that the unrestrained intensification of the *laissez-faire* capitalism and the spread of the market values to all areas of life is endangering our open and democratic society. I believe that the main enemy of the open and democratic society is no longer communism, but the capitalist threat.[17]

Such a vigorous attack, coming from someone at the top of the system, could only cause, as it did, a great deal of controversy. *Forbes* magazine, for instance, published an article about Soros in which it refutes none of his fundamental arguments but limits itself basically to personal criticisms, trying to combat his ideas by demoralizing the author, calling him a rich and eccentric man, and 'a little ridiculous – he spends his time flying the world over, giving press conferences and writing books and articles that no one understands'.[18]

Vargas Llosa, a fierce sponsor of neoliberalism, also wrote an article to refute George Soros, with the suggestive title of 'The Preaching Devil'.[19] In it the author agrees with only one of Soros's theses, that when Adam Smith developed his theory of the invisible hand of the market he was convinced that it was grounded on a very strong moral philosophy and that the great liberal thinkers, including Popper, believed that the market and economic success were just a means for the realization of the lofty ethical ideals of social solidarity as well as of cultural progress and individual betterment. And that in today's version of triumphant capitalism the cult of success replaced the belief in principles, and for that reason society lost its direction.

For him a big challenge to capitalism is today's breakdown of religious culture and a radical transformation of the culture brought about by the development of technology, science and economics. He appeals to the authority of Adam Smith and Von Mises to defend the thesis that an intense cultural and religious life is the 'indispensable complement of the free market for achieving civilization'.[20] The appeal to culture, particularly to religious culture, by ardent sponsors of neoliberalism

---

17 George Soros, 'The capitalist threat', *The Atlantic Monthly*, Feb. 1997, Boston, pp. 45–58. Quoted from p. 45.

18 Reprinted in the *Exame* magazine, no 633 (9 April 1997), p. 99.

19 M. Vargas Llosa, 'O diabo pregador', *O Estado de S. Paulo*, 2 March 1997, São Paulo, p. A-2.

20 Vargas Llosa, 'O diabo pregador'.

is a sign of the times which shows that its victory is not so final and is far less definitive than they would like it to be and used to preach. Incidentally there is a perceptible tendency among liberal economists to re-read Adam Smith, by way of complementing the classic *The Wealth of the Nations* with his other major work, *A Theory of Moral Sentiments*.

This new appreciation of the cultural dimension and even of ethical and religious questions was already noticeable in the field of business administration. The competition of Japanese businesses forced Western businesses to embark on programmes of reorganization such as quality control and re-engineering. In this process they had to deal with ethical, cultural and religious questions. Beside this external influence, there was also an internal cause. With the upsurge of big business and corporations of the incorporated company type capitalism found itself facing a new problem. The growth led to the build-up of a bureaucracy in private businesses, and to the distinction between the owners or stockholders and business managers. These two factors generated the serious problem of corruption in the heart of the businesses. If a high ranking staff person takes individual liberalism – the defense of self-interest – to an extreme inside these businesses, he or she can bankrupt or cause big economic problems for the business, as has been often reported in the media.

These external and internal challenges led to a new appreciation of ethics in business and its transactions,[21] to the extent that today it is obligatory for all major administrative staff of business institutions to take classes on ethics as well as on cultural and religious questions.[22] It is important to highlight that this appreciation of ethics, culture and religion in business administration is instrumental in character, namely, its aim is not ethics or religion, but rather greater productive efficiency.

This change of focus that previously was restricted to the field of business administration is also arriving at the field of economics. The

---

21 See, for intance, Barbara L. Toffler, *Etica no trabalho*, São Paulo, Makron Books, 1993. [English language edn: *Managers Talk Ethics: Making Tough Choices in a Competitive World*, Indianapolis, John Wiley & Son, 1991.] Nash, Laura, *Etica nas empresas*, São Paulo, Makron Books, 1993. [English language edn: *Good Intentions Aside: A Manager's Guide to Resolving Ethical Problems*, Cambridge, Mass., Harvard Business School Press, 1990.]

22 See, for instance, Tom Chappell, *A alma do negócio*, Rio de Janeiro, Campus, 1994. [English language edn: *The Soul of a Business: Managing for Profit and the Common Good*, New York, Bantam Books, 1993.] Stephen R. Covey, *Os sete habitos das pessoas muito eficazes*, 13th edn, São Paulo, Best seller, n.d.

controversy about George Soros and the article by Vargas Llosa are just the tip of the iceberg. For a better understanding of this question let's consider some internal contradictions of the capitalist system which are behind this new appreciation of the culture and religious values in the economy.

The contradictions of the system

Before dealing with the internal contradictions of capitalism, it is important for us to highlight another more concrete sign of the crisis of the capitalist system: the slowing of the rhythm of economic growth.

> In the decade of the 1960s the world economy grew at a rate of 5.0 percent per year after correcting for inflation. In the 1970s growth dropped to 3.6 per cent per year. In the 1980s there was a further deceleration to 2.8 per cent per year, and in the first half of the 1990s the world could manage a growth rate of just 2.0 per cent per year. In two decades capitalism lost 60 per cent of its momentum.[23]

This diagnostic of the crisis is not based on extra-capitalist criteria, such as the exclusion of the poor, but rather in the capitalist criterion *par excellence*, that is, economic growth. This is the main reason why some unconditional defenders of capitalism are proposing a new reading of the economic theory and agreeing to discuss its internal contradictions.

That said, the first contradiction we want to deal with is the one that happens between democracy and the market in the Western capitalist countries. This specification of Western capitalist countries is needed because in the East, particularly in the so-called Asian tiger countries, modernization in the capitalist field was followed neither by political democratization nor by the Western liberal individualism. However, with the strengthening of the market culture 'the Asian societies of Confucian tradition centred in the family are rapidly changing to a self-centred individualism. The restless quest for material success becomes the instrument to measure one's value and position in society.'[24]

In the West the victory over the communist bloc was celebrated as the victory of democratic capitalism. Liberal-democracy is based on the notion of 'one person, one vote', namely, on the formal equality

---

23 Thurow, *Future of Capitalism*, p. 1.
24 Bernardo Teo, 'As religiões orientais e o mercado', *Concilium*, no 270, 1997, Petrópolis, pp. 83–91. Quoted on p. 88.

of all citizens. The market system, on the other hand, is based on the capacity for competition of individuals in the market, on the survival of the strongest or fittest. As such it tends toward social inequality and concentration of wealth, ending up, as in our days, with the social exclusion of an important portion of the population.

In past decades this contradiction was avoided thanks to the welfare state. It was up to the government to shrink the social differences and provide to all citizens, at least in principle, the conditions for a worthy life as well as for the capacity to compete for the available opportunities in the labour market. It is good for us to remember that this model, the welfare state, became a reality in the heart of capitalism, as a result of social pressure and the threat of the socialist alternative. Ruling elites preferred 'to deliver the rings so as not to lose their finger'. With the defeat of the socialist bloc and the hegemony of the neoliberalism, the dismantling of the welfare programme came to be seen as something necessary and useful.

The ideological counterpart of this dismantling was the resurgence of 'social Darwinism' with new 'scientific'[25] clothes and what Galbraith called 'the culture of contentment',[26] where personal wealth is seen as rightfully deserved, and therefore, poverty also as rightful and deserved punishment in view of the inefficiency of the poor, and with that the return of the idea that, if individuals are forced to go hungry, they will do their best to survive in the market. Thus, the end of public assistance to the poor would lead those marginalized by the market to be reintegrated in the market by their own efforts. According to this logic social programmes not only are inefficient and generating of public deficit, but also personally harmful to the poor for not leading them to assume their own responsibility and develop their whole potential.

The problem is that no society can live for long with this cynical culture. A cynical individualism taken to its extreme ends up by destroying the very notion of society. Furthermore, structural unemployment, social exclusion, the dismantling of social programmes and the cynical culture add up to a boiling pot which can result in social rebellion or rupture of the social fabric.

The second contradiction is one that happens between consumption and investment. This tension is implicit in every type of capitalism. As we saw above, it is fundamental in capitalism that individuals believe that they have not only the right but also the duty to make

---

25 A typical example of this tendency is the book of R. J. Herrnstein and C. Murray, *The Bell Curve*, New York, Free Press, 1994.

26 John Kenneth Galbraith, *The Culture of Contentment*, Wilmington, Houghton Mifflin, 1992.

the maximum of money so as to enjoy better and better consumption patterns. The problem is that in order to be able to offer better and better patterns, capitalism has to see that these same individuals restrain their desire for consumption and leisure and invest money and time in new factories, equipment, infra-structure and research and development of new technologies as well as in workers' training.

In the past this contradiction was in part solved by the secular puritanical ascetism that was 'powerfully against the spontaneous enjoyment of possessions; it restricted consumption, especially of luxuries. On the other hand, it had the psychological effect of freeing the acquisition of goods from the inhibitions of traditionalist ethics,'[27] thus bursting the shackles of anxiety. This work ethic was being slowly replaced by the consumption ethic. However, during the Cold War, government had an important function of investment in new technologies, especially in the military area, which worked as the lever of economic development in capitalist countries.

Today, in this era of business based on intellectual capacity, the investment in the human abilities of the population in general, in technology and in the infrastructure, is a key requirement of sustainable economic growth. The problem is that individuals and capitalist businesses, due to their own internal logic cannot by themselves be responsible for this type of investment in the long run. This task of representing the atomized interests of businesses and individuals and to make the needed investments for the future of capitalism is up to government. However, with the end of the Cold War, the hegemony of neoliberalism, with its minimal government programme and the individualist culture with its consumer ethic, are taking the states into reverse, that is the immediate consumption of funds on behalf of today's citizen voters, and, in the case of the Latin American countries, to use them to pay the interest on the internal and external debts and to finance the fascination with imported consumer goods.

In the particular case of the Latin American countries, one needs to be reminded that the problem of the external debt, in spite of media silence on the topic, continues to be a big obstacle for the development of the region. As Bresser Pereira says, 'currently, the main restriction to growth comes from the characteristic imbalances that persist for the long run, induced by the crisis of the external debt, which did not reverse itself, even after ten years.'[28] For him,

---

27 Max Weber, *The Protestant Ethic*, p. 171.
28 Luiz Carlos Bresser Pereira, *Crise econômicae reforma do Estado no Brasil. Para uma nova interpretação da América Latina*, São Paulo, Ed. 34, 1996, p. 46.

growth will be retaken only if the stabilization and the market oriented reforms were complemented by the recovering of the state's capacity for saving and by the development of policies that define a new strategic role for the state. In other words, provided that the state be rebuilt, recovering its capacity for intervention.[29]

Irrespective of his thesis regarding market orientation and possible identification of economic growth and social development, the record shows the fundamental importance of rebuilding the capacity for intervention by the state in the economic and social fields. Without that neither the economic crisis in most Latin American countries nor the contradictions of capitalism (regarding consumption and investment), and much less the grave problem of social exclusion, will be solved.

At this point it is worth including a long quote from Lester Thurow:

Technology and ideology are shaking the foundations of twenty-first-century capitalism. Technology is making skills and knowledge the only sources of sustainable strategic advantage. Abetted by the electronic media, ideology is moving toward a radical form of short-run individual consumption at precisely a time when economic success will depend upon the willingness and ability to make lung-run social investments in skills, education, knowledge and infrastructure. When technology and ideology start moving apart, the only question is when will the 'big one' (the earthquake that rocks the system) occur. Paradoxically, at precisely the time when capitalism finds itself with no social competitors – its former competitors, socialism or communism, having died – it will have to undergo a profound metamorphosis.[30]

'In the era ahead capitalism will have to create new values and new institutions.'[31]

It is good to keep in mind that the author of this affirmation is no socialist or Marxist who insists on foreseeing the imminent end of capitalism, but rather a respected MIT professor of economics; and that this crisis of capitalism is neither 'about to arrive', as many would like to see it, nor is it a 'final crisis'. However, I believe that this is something the defenders of capitalism are concerned about. It is in this sense that we can interpret the affirmation of Vargas Llosa that 'this is

---

29 Bresser Pereira, *Crise econômicae*, p. 52.
30 Thurow, *Spirit of Capitalism*, p. 326
31 Thurow, *Spirit of Capitalism*, p. 309.

a challenge that the open societies will have to deal with and for which none of them has found yet a creative response'.

Religion and economics

In the face of these problems we find two types of attitude. One of them denies their seriousness or importance and maintains an unshakable faith in the market's capacity to solve by unconscious automatism all social and economic problems. Paul Ormerod says that, in the face of the world economy which is in crisis – with the number of unemployed nearing 20 million in Western Europe, and the United States facing the grave problem of budget deficits and trade balance, with the Japanese companies about to break with the tradition of employment for life due to the deepest recession since the war, and with big portions of the former Soviet Union nearing economic collapse – 'orthodox economic theory, trapped in an idealized and mechanistic view of the world, is powerless to assist'. He also points out that the economists of the International Monetary Fund and the World Bank, protected and secure by their bureaucracies, 'preach salvation through the market to the Third World'.[32]

'The believers in the redeeming virtues of globalized capitalism'[33]for their own faith in the market, end up caught in a trap. Faith in the capacity of the market's 'invisible hand' to transform unintentionally the sum total of self-interest into common good leaves no room for the search for a solution of the crisis outside the market logic. To search for extra-market solutions, such as intervention by government or civil society would be a denial of faith in the market. From the perspective of this faith, all social problems are seen as 'necessary sacrifices' demanded by the market. This transcendentalizing of the market and the resulting sacrificialism are criticized by the Liberation Theologians as the market's idolatry.[34] The Western notion of 'necessary sacrifices' is strongly influenced by Christianity's interpretation of the death of Jesus. By interpreting the death of Jesus as a definitive and full sacrificial death demanded by God the Father for the salvation of human-

---

32 Ormerod, *Death of Economics*, p. 3.

33 Luiz Gonzaga Bellyzzo, 'A globalização da estupidez', *Caarta Capital*, 18 Sept. 1996, year 3, no 32, São Paulo, p. 59. This expression is interesting because it comes not from a liberation theologian, but from an economist.

34 H. Assmann and F. Hinkelammert, *Idolatria do Mercado*, Petrópolis, Vozes, 1989; H. Assmann, *Crítica à lógica da exclusão*, São Paulo, Paulus, 1995; J. M. Sung, *Deus numa economia sem coração*, 2nd edn, São Paulo, Paulus, 1994; *Teologia e economia*, 2nd edn, Petrópolis, Vozes, 1995.

kind, Christianity ended up by consolidating the idea that there is no salvation without sacrifice.

This theology implies a transfiguration of evil. When suffering imposed on human beings is considered as a way of salvation demanded by God, it ceases to be an evil and becomes a 'good' from which we could not and should not want to flee. This inversion, typical of idolatry, has the power of generating consciences unconcerned with the problem of human suffering.[35] That is what we previously called the 'culture of cynicism'. This type of sacrificial theology was useful, for instance, in justifying the sacrifice of millions of indigenous people in the Americas. It is useful as well to theologians like M. Novak who criticize theologies and communities in the struggle to lessen the suffering of the poor, saying: 'If God so willed his beloved Son to suffer, why would He spare us?'[36]

In the market's logic human sacrifices are no longer demanded in the name of a transcendental God, but in the name of an institution that was transendentalized, namely, the market. The sacrifices, the social costs, are imposed on human beings in the name of economic redemption. When these sacrifices do not generate the promised results, their sponsors are left with two options: to accept that the sacrifices were in vain and acknowledge responsibility for mass murder or to defend themselves by saying that the sacrifices have not been effective because there are still many people and groups who persist in not accepting the inevitability of the market laws and demand intervention in the market through social movements, labour unions, political parties and other institutions as well as intervention in the market aiming at social goals.

In practice this group aims at solving the above mentioned contradictions by relativizing and even despising democracy, united with the culture of cynicism and social exclusion and with a time vision restricted to the present, that is, to current consumption, believing in the magic capacity of the market and in the infinite capacity of technology.

George Gilder, a famous American consultant, is a typical example of the mix of religious mysticism, irrationalism and belief in the market and technology that tries to deny the reality of the social contradictions and crisis. Commenting on the contradiction between

---

35 On sacrificial logic and circuit in the West, see Franz Hinkelammert, *Sacrifícios humanos y sociedad occidental: Lucifer y la Bestia*, San José (Costa Rica), DEI, 1991 (Brazilian translation by Ed. Paulus).

36 Michael Novak, *The Spirit of Democratic Capitalism*, New York, Simon & Schuster, 1982, p. 1982.

desire and limitless accumulation and consumption and the limitation of nature he asks: 'Why is it that while human possibilities expand almost boundlessly, many intellectuals feel only new pangs of claustrophobia?' He responds:

> The contemporary intellectual denying God, is in a trap, and he projects his entrapment onto the world. But the world is not entrapped; man is not finite; the human mind is not bound in material brain. Like most of the hype and hysterics of modern intellectuals, the energy crisis is most essentially a religious disorder, a failure of faith. It can be overcome chiefly by worship: by a recognition that beyond the darkness and opacity of our material entrapment is a realm of redemptive spirit, reachable through that interplay of faith and fact which some call science, others poetry, but which is most luminously comprehended as forms of prayer.[37]

This long quote may enrapture religious people who naively believe that any reference to religion, especially in such a mystical language, is, in itself, good. This religious speech which sounds like so many others that flood the so much heralded revalorization of spirituality today is nothing but a speech that tries to deny the real contradiction between the desire of limitless consumption and the limitations of both the human being and nature as a whole. This negation implies the real possibility of destruction of the human *habitat* and condemnation of a great part of the human population to the condition of sub-human life.[38]

A second position assumes the gravity of the contradictions and of the economic crisis and looks for an exit not exclusively from the inner logic of the market but subordinated to it. Francis Fukuyama, the famous author of the thesis of the 'end of history', takes this position with his book, *Trust – The Social Virtues and the Creation of Prosperity*. In it he affirms that greater economic efficiency is not obtained by self-interested rational individuals but rather by groups of individuals who are capable of working efficiently together, due to a pre-existing moral community. For him 'one of the most important lessons we can learn from an examination of economic life is that a nation's well-

---

37 G. Gilder, *The Spirit of Enterprise*, New York, Simon & Schuster, 1984, pp. 69–70.

38 On the problem of ecology and its relation with the poor, see L. Boff, *Ecologia: grito da Terra, grito dos pobres*, São Paulo, Ática, 1995. [English language edn: *Cry of the Earth, Cry of the Poor*, Maryknoll, NY, Orbis Books, 1997.]

being, and its ability to compete, are conditioned by a single, pervasive cultural characteristic: the *level* of trust inherent in the society.'[39]

According to Kenneth J. Arrow, Nobel Prize winner in Economics, 'trust has a very important pragmatic value, if nothing else. . . . It is extremely efficient; it saves a lot of trouble to have a fair degree of reliance on other people's word. Unfortunately this is not a commodity which can be bought very easily.'[40] If, 'unfortunately', confidence is not yet a commodity available in the market, where else may one obtain such a fundamental component for economic efficiency? Fukuyama answers: 'trust is not a consequence of rational calculation; it arises from sources like religion or ethical habits, that have nothing to do with modernity'.[41] Thus he sponsors the view that 'if the institutions of democracy and capitalism are to work properly, they must coexist with certain pre-modern cultural habits that ensure their proper functioning'. And these 'are not anachronisms in a modern society but rather the sine qua non of the latter's success'.[42]

This recovering of premodern values, particularly religious values, is not a dismissal of the thesis that capitalism is the apex of history, but rather a retaking of a North American tradition. As Michael Albert says,

> since its beginnings, no doubt, America has been devoted to the dollar, but kept one hand on the Bible and another on the constitution. It remained a deeply religious society . . . And the traditional moral implied restrictions, inspired commandments which were not simply formal . . . And as for the 'associative fabric' so full of life, it has already been said how important its role as social softener was. To summarize, by administering its basic contradictions the American Society used to find its balance. It is precisely this balance that is disrupted today. Money was king but, as in the case of all majesties, its power was contained; it was limited. Today, its power tends to invade all social activities.[43]

This rupture, or in the words of Robert Reich, former Secretary of

---

39 F. Fukuyama, *Trust – The Social Virtues and the Creation of Prosperity*, New York, The Free Press, 1995, p. 7.

40 Kenneth J. Arrow, *The Limits of Organization*, quoted in Fukuyama, *Trust*, pp. 151–2.

41 Fukuyama, *Trust*, p. 352.

42 Fukuyama, *Trust*, p. 11.

43 Michel Albert, *Capitalismo vs. capitalismo*, São Paulo, Fundação Fides-Loyola, 1992, p. 102. [English edn: *Capitalism against Capitalism*, London, Whurr, 1993.]

Labor in the Clinton Administration, the disintegration of the social contract, threatens the stability and moral authority of the nation,[44] and that shakes confidence and, in the end, efficiency.

This attempt to revalue religion (its rituals, moral values, myths) as a means for increasing efficiency and competitiveness is easily observable in the literature of business administration and begins to be even more visible in the area of the economy. The previously implicit relation between economics and religion that became visible only after the work to unmask its 'endogenous theology' (Hugo Assmann), is now explicitly sponsored by the very sponsors of the capitalist system.[45]

Both neoliberals and those who acknowledge the need for some type of correction for the maintenance of the current economic system make use of religion: the first group, with its sacrificial and dogmatic discourse; and the second with their pursuit of religion as a way to increase efficiency and to overcome or bypass the internal contradictions of capitalism. Religion is in fashion and will remain so for a long time, not only in the personal and subjective but also in the managerial and macroeconomic spheres.

Transcendence and the market

The religious experience is the experience of a mystery that transcends the human being, whether understood as an experience of the sacred that provokes fascination and fear, as scholars of religion have characterized it,[46] or as an absolutely unique experience that founds a radical meaning for all existence, what mystics call the experience of God.[47] It does not matter here which sense is given to the term

---

44 Robert B. Reich, 'Um programa inacabado', *O Estado de S. Paulo*, 23 Feb. 1997, São Paulo, p. A-2.

45 It is worth quoting as another meaningful example the two lectures by M. Camdessus, managing director of the IMF about the relationship of the Kingdom of God and the market, 'Marché-Royaume. La double appartenence', *Documents Episcopat. Bulletin du Secrétariat de la Conférence des Évêques de France*, no 12, Jul.–Aug. 1992; *Mercado e o Reino frente à globalização da economia mundial*, São Paulo, Newswork, n.d. (presented in Mexico, on 29 October 1993), as shown in Chapter l.

46 Rudolf Otto, *The Idea of the Holy. An Inquiry into the Non-rational Factor in the Idea of the Divine and its Relation to the Rational*, London, New York, Toronto, Oxford University Press, 1950; Mircea Eliade, *O sagrado e o profano*, Lisboa, ed. Livros do Brasil, n.d. [English language edn: *The Sacred and the Profane: The Nature of Religion*, New York, Harvest Books, 1959.]

47 For a differentiation between the religious experience and the experience of God, see Henrique C. de Lima Vaz, 'A experiência de Deus', in (various authors), *Experimentar Deus hoje*, Petrópolis, Vozes, 1974, pp. 74–89.

'religious experience', nor does the veracity of this experience or of the religions, which are necessary institutionalizations realized by social groups that are formed around this type of experience.

In this sense religion is, above all, a human attempt to act out inside history a mystery which is beyond history, which is transcendent. Even a religious discourse with the explicit intention of manipulation must necessarily make mention of a mystery or of beings that transcend the human being. What concerns us here is that the mention of religion necessarily implies, by its own internal logic, a reference to something that is beyond our human reality or our human institutions.

The pretence of revaluing religion as a way to generate confidence or other objectives aiming at increasing efficiency, and in the last resort, at increasing wealth, deprives religion of what is most germane to it: its recourse to transcendence and, therefore, its relativization of all human institutions. The use of religion, or the reduction of religion as an instrument of economic accumulation is only possible and understandable with the absolutization of something that is external to the religious experience and wholly human: the market. The logic of the market, with its law of competition and the survival of the most effective, is then elevated to the condition of an absolute that supports the whole system. Even religion would have to abdicate its recourse to transcendence, of that which is beyond the market and all human institutions to serve this absolute. The market is then transcendentalized, that is, raised to the condition of absolute super-human. It is the idol. This instrumental use of religion reveals, by the very contradiction of its speech, its falsehood and perversity.

Over against the idolatry of the market we must reaffirm our mission: to be witnesses of the resurrection of Jesus; to be announcers of the God of Jesus. The best way of denying the transcendentalization of the market that sacrifices the poor is to witness that God, even while present in the world, is not identified with the world or with any other institution, because God is wholly transcendent. In this sense it is very important for us to make it clear that the Church's mission is a religious mission.

To say that the mission of the Church is religious does not mean to say that the Church and the Christians should not interact with economic, social and political questions. If that were the case, we would be witnesses of a God totally insensitive to the suffering of human beings: the contrary of the God who is love and mercy. This means that the actions and proclamations of the Christian churches must maintain their religious specificity, namely, to act and speak from the standpoint our faith experience.

Even in a modern society, believed to be a secularized one, and even inside the parameters of modern critical reason, there is a fundamental task for the religions: to announce God's transcendence so that human beings will not forget their human condition and thus to prevent the absolutizing of any social institution. Horkheimer reminds us very well that 'any limited being – and humankind is limited – that considers itself as the ultimate, the highest and the unique, converts itself into an idol which hungers for blood sacrifices, besides having the demonic capacity of changing its identity and assigning different meaning to things'.[48] It happens that, with this sense of danger, we cannot counterpose a corroboration of the existence of God, since the 'conscious knowledge of destitution, of our finitude, cannot be considered as the proof of God's existence, but only produce the *hope* that a positive absolute does exist'. This does not mean that we should not talk about the absolute, for if we cannot represent the absolute with our human language, we can, when talking about the absolute, affirm that 'the world in which we live is something relative'.[49] In this sense, for Horkheimer theology is not a speech about God as God in Godself, but

the consciousness that the world is a phenomenon, that it is neither the absolute nor the ultimate truth. Theology is – I express myself consciously and with prudence – the hope that the injustice that characterizes the world cannot remain as such; that what is unrighteous cannot consider itself as the last word.[50]

To be witnesses of God's transcendence is not an easy task. The very structure of the religious experience is marked by the possibility of idolatry. Since due to our condition we can have experience with the sacred only through something human, be it an object or the moral law, we always run the risk of mistaking this human 'support' for the very transcendent mystery. This is what often happens when we forget that the sacraments, religious rituals and the Church are never pure and full manifestations of God, when we forget that the Church or our social project for the poor are not the Kingdom of God, and therefore cannot be absolutized, but rather always criticized and 'reformed'. Idolatry is not something that happens only in the market, but rather a permanent temptation in all human groups.

---

48 Max Horkheimer, 'La añoranza de lo completamente otro', in H. Marcuse, K. Popper and M. Horkheimer, *A la búsqueda del sentido*, Salamanca, Sígueme, 1976, pp. 67–124. Quoted on p. 68.
49 Horkheimer, 'La añoranza', p. 103.
50 Horkheimer, 'La añoranza', p. 106.

One way to overcome the temptation of idolatry is always to affirm the absolute transcendence of God, but, as Jon Sobrino says, 'if on the one hand the transcendent nature of the experience of God and the eschatological reserve prohibits declaring only one exclusive place for the experience of God, on the other hand they do not demand the relativizing of any historical place in relation to such experience.'[51] The place *par excellence* where we can have the experience with God in history and at the same time the place to criticize radically the idolatry of the market is in the midst of the poor, the excluded from the system that absolutizes itself. The market system in its attempt of self-absolutizing has to deny other forms of thinking, namely, it has to impose a 'single thinking', denying any social alternative other than capitalism and denying the existence of persons outside the system. For the existence of a different thinking, a social or personal alternative that is not part of this system, exposes its relativity and limits. With its hegemony in the ideological field and the media, it is not difficult to deny the existence and vitality of alternative thinking and projects. But it is difficult to deny the existence of groups of people who are out of the market, that is, more than one billion people in the world.

There are basically two ways of denying the limitations exposed by the excluded. The first is to say as indeed the priests of the market do, that unfortunately the market still has not become really total, but that the necessary and beneficient expansion of the market in all aspects of life and all over the world will solve this problem. In the end it is the thesis that the market has not yet resolved all the problems because it has not yet become all in all. The second is to deny the human dignity of those who were excluded from the market. Since they are individuals without human dignity, due to their inefficiency and 'laziness', there is no one outside the market able to reveal the market's limitations and relativity. Usually we come across a combination of these two arguments.

To affirm the existence of the excluded, the fundamental dignity of them all, and to hear their clamour[52] and to witness – with the visible presence of the Church in the midst of the poor and in concrete struggles on their behalf – that God is among them, is the best way of deny-

---

51 Jon Sobrino, *A resurreição da verdadeira Igreja*, São Paulo, Loyola, 1982, p. 138.

52 On the revelation, the clamour of the poor and the market see J. M. Sung, *Deus numa economia sem coração;* and H. Assmann, *Clamor dos pobres e racionalidade econômica*, São Paulo, Paulus, 1991. In the philosophical perspective, the theme of the excluded as the 'other' of the market system was extensively dealt with by E. Dussel.

ing the absolutizing of the market, of unveiling concretely and practically its limits. However to deny the idolatry of the market and to show its limits is not to deny the market in an absolute way – that would be reverse idolatry. What we need is an adjustment of the market in line with the objective of a dignified and enjoyable life for all human beings. And, for that, the option for the poor, with all that it means, continues to be a privileged way for Church and Christians in their mission of witnessing their faith in the God who wishes 'that they may have life, and have it abundantly' (John 10.10).

Another important point of our mission is the problem of sacrifice. The idol is the God who demands human sacrifices, who does not forgive or hear the clamours of the poor. God, on the contrary, is the One that does hear the clamours, and instead of demanding sacrifices, offers mercy as a gift.

We know that the market 'absorbed' its sacrificial theology from a determined historical configuration of Christianity. It is obvious that sacrificialism was and is present in many other religions and societies. The influence of the Christian sacrificial theology in the mentality of the West is also undeniable. In the struggle against the culture of insensitivity that marks our time, it is fundamental that we show that human suffering, particularly the suffering of the poor and excluded by an oppressive and unjust economic system is not a part of God's demand for salvation. We need, with our living practices and witness to show that what God wants 'is mercy, not sacrifices' (Matt. 9.13).

As Juan Luis Segundo always insisted, there cannot be a Liberation Theology without a liberation of theology. We will not be able effectively to contribute to the struggle against the social exclusion caused by the current system of market without being able at the same time to free ourselves from the sacrificial logic that prevails in many of our theologies of salvation.

Finally, I want to highlight that these theological-political principles, that is, the transcendence of God that denies the absolutizing of the market and the critique of sacrificialism in the name of mercy, belong in the field of ideological debate. It is an important debate, but it should not make us forget that there is another pole: the one of the technology and institutions. Our spirituality must not only unmask the neoliberal ideology that cements the prevailing excluding system, but also must contribute to the formulation of new guidelines for the creation of new institutions and techniques. In the tension between these two poles it is fundamental for us to remember that God, the plenitude, the absolute, is always beyond our human and historical possibilities. In other words, our experience of the mystery of God and our desire to see the problems of our brothers and sisters fully and definitely resolved, should not let us forget that it is in the midst of the historical limitations and possibilities that we can build not the Kingdom of God, but societies and institutions that, in spite of all ambiguities and limitations, in being more just and brotherly and sisterly ones, may also be anticipatory signs of the definitive Kingdom.

5

Liberation Theology between the Desire for Abundance and the Reality of Scarcity

Gustavo Gutiérrez, speaking at the *Conference on Christianity in Latin America and the Caribbean*, held in the city of São Paulo from 29 July to 1 August in 2003, said: 'Liberation Theology did not die! If it died, I was not invited to the burial.' The audience reacted with applause and delight. The conference, with massive participation of people from many parts of Brazil and Latin America, was, for many, a confirmation that Latin American Liberation Theology (LALT) still continues alive and necessary.

However, we must be clear that a theology does not die because somebody wrote that it is deceased nor remain alive because a group desires that it continue to live. A theological tradition is kept alive and relevant to the extent that it has a group of people producing theological texts and reflections in which they are answering new challenges and overcoming imperfections and problems, conjunctural or structural, in their tradition of thought.

The maintenance of the option for the poor for many ecclesial communities and Christian groups is basic, but by itself this does not guarantee the continuity of LALT, much less the persistence of the oppression of the majority of the population, victims of unjust economic and social structures and of ethnic relations and gender oppression. The reality of oppression and the practice of resistance and/or of liberation are necessary starting points, the first moment, but do not guarantee the continuity and the social and ecclesial relevance of LALT.

I am not going to argue here whether or not LALT is deceased or revisit the debates on the main epistemological problems and challenges of LALT.[1] But I think that this or other theologies that claim

---

1 There are already a reasonable number of books concerning the problems

to be at the service of the life and dignity of the world's victims will remain alive and relevant only to the extent that we manage to prepare pertinent and relevant reflections beginning with and concerning the questions and problems that are born from the struggle of the groups and people committed to the life and dignity of our suffering people.

As Gustavo Gutiérrez said in the early years of LALT:

> Theology must be a way of thinking critical of itself, of its foundations. . . . But not only in this aspect, of epistemological character, we allude to the speech of theology as critical reflection. We also refer to a discerning and critical attitude in relation to the economic and socio-cultural conditionings of the life and reflection of the Christian community . . . Moreover, and most of all, however, we take that expression as the theory of a definite practice. Theological reflection would be, then, necessarily, a critique of society and the Church while called and addressed by the word of God; a critical theory in the light of the word accepted in faith and inspired by a practical purpose, and therefore indissolubly linked to historical praxis.[2]

The notion that theology is the 'second moment', which is born in and at the service of the practice of liberation is, without a doubt, one of the basic characteristics of LALT. In affirming itself as the second moment, LALT explicitly assumes that its reflections will be attempts to answer, in the first place, the questions born of ethical indignation and the struggles in facing situations of oppression, and not answer the questions placed by mere theoreticians for the academic world, whether of the First or Third World. In other words, the agenda of LALT would have to be dictated by ecclesial, social, and political movements preoccupied with 'discovering and proclaiming the deeper meaning' of their struggles and of historical events.[3] Clearly this does not mean abandoning dialogue with the academic world, but subordinating the agenda of that dialogue to the priorities arising from praxis.

---

and perspectives of Liberation Theology. For example, L. C. Susin (ed.), *O mar se abriu: trinta anos de teologia na América Latina*, São Paulo, Loyola, 2000; Idem (ed.), *Sarça Ardente: teologia na América Latina: prospectivas*, São Paulo, Paulinas, 2000; J. Duque (ed.), *Perfiles teológicos para un nuevo milenio*, San José (Costa Rica), DEI-CETELA, 1997; J. M. Sung, *Teologia e economia: repensando a TL e utopias*, Petrópolis, Vozes, 1994.

2 G. Gutiérrez, *Teologia da Libertação*. Perspectivas, 6th edn, Petrópolis, Vozes, 1986, p. 23. [English language edn: *A Theology of Liberation*, trans. Caridad Inda and John Eagleson, Maryknoll, NY, Orbis Books, 1973.]

3 Gutiérrez, *Teologia*, p. 25.

Assuming this epistemological principle of LALT, I want in this chapter to consider some provisory reflections beginning with two facts or problems.

New praxis, new challenges, and new problems

In a course promoted by the CESEP (Ecumenical Center of Services for Evangelization and Popular Education),[4] a leader of a popular organization from Argentina presented the following problem. She, along with other people of a Catholic ecclesial community, after coming into contact with Liberation Theology, had undertaken diverse works of awareness and organization of the people of its quarter. After many struggles, coming and going, in the midst of which 'the liberation of the poor' did not arrive, they created a co-operative of production and consumption to improve the conditions of life of the people of the quarter. The struggle was no longer centred on the theme of liberation, but in the improvement of the daily life of the people. When the co-operative was formed, the direction was constituted, as was expected, by the leadership of the movement.

On the occasion of the course, the co-operative was going reasonably well, but it faced a serious problem: one of the directors, who had been one of the first and more important leaders of the popular movement that gave rise to the co-operative, was not being efficient in his job. He was a good leader, binding people together and mobilizing them, but he did not have the ability necessary to manage an economic organization like a co-operative. Other members of the board knew that the co-operative was not in a financial position to pay an inefficient director nor to shoulder the costs of this director's mismanagement; but, at the same time, they did not want the criterion of efficiency to subordinate the criterion of solidarity with a longstanding leader. Therefore, for them, to allow themselves to be led by the criterion of efficiency would be to assume neoliberalism, which they had criticized so much. However, they were also aware that the future of the co-operative was in jeopardy.

In cases like this, it is not enough to criticize neoliberalism and proclaim solidarity, the option for the poor, or the right of all to a life of dignity. It is necessary to find concrete solutions, to decide before the

---

4 The 'Curso para militantes cristãos latino-americanos' (Course for Latin-American Christian Activists) with a duration of four weeks, held in the month of May in São Paulo, congregating around 35 leaders from all over Latin America and the Caribbean, including Cuba. For more information: http://www.cesep.org.br/.

problem becomes greater and places this popular organization at risk. What does one do when experiencing such a conflict in the administration of a popular project? Is it being neoliberal to use the criterion of economic efficiency in this case and to keep the co-operative functioning well? Must one run the risk of the co-operative entering economic collapse in order to maintain the identity of an established enterprise based only in solidarity? The member who had presented the problem was aware that one would not have to decide only according to the criteria of efficiency presented by theories of business administration, but, at the same time, was also convinced that one could not simply act in the name of solidarity leaving aside altogether the criterion of administrative efficiency.

A second example: at the fifth Ministerial Conference of the World Trade Organization (WTO) held in Cancún, Mexico, in September 2003, a new fact in the international scene appeared. A group of 22 developing countries – among them South Africa, Brazil, China, and India – acted together to demand from the rich countries a reduction in the agricultural subsidies that they grant to their producers and the elimination of tariff and non-tariff barriers on the products exported from developing countries, like food and textiles. The novelty of the formation and joint performance of this group was so outstanding that James Wolfensohn, president of the World Bank, came to affirm in an interview that the G-22 marked the creation of 'a new paradigm in the global financial relations of the twenty-first century'.[5]

The G-22, also known as G-20 Plus, represents about 63 per cent of the world's farmers, 51 per cent of the global population, and 20 per cent of global agricultural production. The non-rich countries exporting agricultural products are harmed by the protectionist schemes that the rich countries give to their agricultural producers and exporters. The agricultural subsidies of the rich countries, which reach US $360 billion per year, depreciate the prices of agricultural products to such a point that they impede the substantive reduction of the misery and poverty in many poor countries. An example of the perverse consequence of this policy: according to the World Bank, if the price of cotton on the international market was not lowered by the subsidies of rich countries, the number of poor people in the African country of Burkina Faso would be cut in half in six years.

Beyond those subsidies, the tariff barriers of the rich countries produce the paradox of poor countries paying more taxes on international

---

5 Interview given to *The Wall Street Journal Américas*, published in *O Estado de São Paulo*, São Paulo, 18 September 2003, p. B-16.

trade than rich countries. According to studies presented in the *Oxfam Policy Papers*, the United States, for example, imposes tariffs that vary from 0 to 1 per cent for the main products imported from Great Britain, France, Japan, and Germany, while it taxes from 14 to 15 per cent products that arrive from Bangladesh, Cambodia, and Nepal.[6]

The reason for those subsidies and tariff barriers is that the farmers in non-developed countries are more competitive than those in rich countries. That is, in order to defend the farmers of their own countries and also the industrial sectors less competitive in relation to the non-developed countries, such as the textile sector, rich countries impose policies that make difficult, not to say almost impossible, the economic development and overcoming of poverty of non-developed countries.

In the face of a factual situation where the logic of the free market is enforced in economic sectors where the rich countries possess advantages in relation to the poor (high-technology products and the financial market) and where they enforce subsidies and barriers against the trade of products where the advantage is with the non-rich countries, there are basically two possible responses: economic isolation, that is, non-participation in international trade of the non-developed countries, or the struggle for the liberalization of international trade in these sectors. Isolation is not viable because the non-developed countries do not possess the technology or scales of production necessary to produce at a reasonable cost all the necessary goods (such as antibiotics, fertilizers, computers, communication systems, modes of mass transport, oil and its derivatives, etc.) for the reproduction of the life of the society. One possible idea – to impose barriers to imported products from rich countries – faces political difficulties (if this were not difficult, the neoliberals would not have managed to impose free trade in this sector on almost the whole world), beyond raising the cost of the production of goods necessary for internal consumption and for export. All that remains then is the struggle for the liberalization of all the segments of international trade! This is the reason why President Lula declared: 'See that we, at no point, are asking for any benefit of privilege or for any favour. What we are asking is that the developed countries make a policy of foreign trade where we are treated as equals. We only want the opportunity to compete freely.'[7]

---

6 Available on the Internet: www.oxfam.org.uk.

7 Cited in the news publication *In Question*, the electronic bulletin edited by the Secretaria de Comunicação de Governo and Gestão Estratégica da Presidência da República (The General Office of Government Communication and Strategic Management of the Presidency of the Republic), no 77, from 18 September 2003.

For many who have criticized the Lula government as a neoliberal government, this declaration would be one more proof of its conversion to neoliberalism.[8] After all, the defence of free trade was always a sign of neoliberalism and the sectors identified with the poor have always criticized that proposal. Might it be that the Lula government, like the government of the Chinese Communist Party and G-22 governments with social-democratic tendencies, has abandoned its ideological option for the working classes or social commitment and has assumed the 'idolatry of the neoliberal market'? If yes, must we who participated and contributed in one way or another to the election of the first president of working-class origin in Brazil, and all those that had shared the hope of a country more socially just with a popular government, assume a position of explicit opposition to the government for having abandoned its origins and popular causes and for walking arm in arm with neoliberal 'idolaters of the market'?

These questions concerning faith and administrative resolutions, efficiency and solidarity in popular organizations, or the paradox of a popular government accepting apparently neoliberal banners of struggle, are recent questions and the products of popular victories. In the 1970s and 80s, LALT did not debate questions like these for a simple reason: they were not questions posed by ecclesial and social practices. It was the advance and achievements of popular struggles that brought about these new questions. These questions would not have appeared if people and groups that had dedicated precious time in their lives to conscientization and the organization of people in the struggle for the liberation of the poor had given up with the delay of liberation or were even faced with the awareness of the impossibility of that liberation. It was necessary that many Christians and people of good will should overcome the disenchantment similar to that of the disciples of Emmaus: 'We were hoping he was the one who would redeem Israel . . .' (Luke 24.21). These new questions arose from perseverance in the struggle despite the frustration of the great hope that the poor of Jesus, finally, would be free from oppressions. Liberation had been conceived

---

8 For example, Ivo Lesbaupin, in the text, 'Governo Lula: neoliberal?' ('The Lula Administration: Neoliberal?'), June 2003, much circulated on the Internet, affirms: 'In the last eight years, I dedicated myself to demystify the propaganda of the Fernando Henrique Cardoso administration and to denounce the neoliberal character of its policies, as well as the ominous consequences of the same. For what reason was welfare reform chosen by the current government as its reform priority? It was a priority for the FHC administration, which managed to carry part of it through; not managing to realize the part regarding public servants. The Lula administration took for itself the task of carrying it out. *All neoliberal governments have welfare reform as a basic task.*'

on the one hand 'as overcoming all slavery; and on the other, as a vocation to be new men, creators of a new world'.[9]

The transition or passage from struggles merely contestatory and demanding of the State to the creation and management of popular organizations, like the co-operative, and/or the conquests of elective offices in the legislative or executive powers – on the municipal, state, and federal level – is what these new struggles have made to appear. Those questions only appear at the level of administration and operations – either in the private, public, or in the third sector.

One basic qualitative difference when one passes from a demanding or contestatory movement in the direction of an organization or administration of public power is the necessity of managing scarcity. When we struggle for the liberation of the poor and all humanity, when we desire the New World and the New Human Being, we are dreaming of an environment of abundance, without scarcity, of full freedom, dreaming of the day, as it is sung in the communities, 'in which all upon raising up the vision; we will see in this land the reign of freedom'. But, when we create or participate in organizations, like cooperatives or NGOs, or the institutions of the state, we perceive that we do not have all the time that we would desire, nor all the human, financial, and material resources and political power that we need, nor all the knowledge. In the face of scarcity we will not manage to do everything that we want or think to be necessary. Scarcity limits what we can do. Because of this limit, it is necessary to establish priorities so that we can make decisions. And when we establish priorities, there will always be somebody or some problem at the end of the line, or even outside the line, that will not be taken care of.

Priorities are always established from a criterion. The criterion, in turn, is an ethical-political decision. Having made the ethical-political decision to determine the criteria, priorities must be established and hierarchized and the execution gets into an area where the technical aspect is basic. Without the problem of scarcity the controllers of the co-operative would not need to face the decision to fire or not fire an inefficient friend, and neither would the anti-neoliberal governments of the G-22 face the decision of assuming or not assuming the banner of free trade.

These two examples situate themselves at the extremes in terms of social and geographic contexts: the microeconomic-social level of the co-operative and macroeconomic level of international trade in a

---

9 Leonardo Boff, *Teologia do cativeiro e da libertação*, 2nd edn, Petrópolis, Vozes, 1980, p. 19.

globalized economy. Struggles and decisions, despite the difference in scale, face the paradoxes that emerge from the contradictions of reality and have to do with the concrete lives of the people who suffer from economic and social problems. In a world as complex and large as the current one, the economic relations of the micro-level are articulated and being influenced by actions and situations at the global level. This is the reason why the struggle for a more dignified life for all people, the option for the poor, must face challenges simultaneously on these two levels and also on the other intermediate levels.

In the face of these contradictions and the complexity of reality, there are people and groups that prefer to maintain the purity of their ethical, political, and even theological principles, and are not taking into account the reality of scarcity. Others prefer only to focus on technical aspects, as if the establishment of priorities were not an ethical-theological-political question. There are also people and groups that do not want to lose the sense of reality when faced with scarcity, nor lose sight of the motivation of faith that brought them to the struggle and these situations: people and groups who want to find a deeper and spiritual meaning amid the difficult decisions and contradictions of the real world.

We are not going to discuss in this chapter how the co-operative must decide on the future of its director or whether or not the Lula government is a neoliberal government. But, I think that we must recognize that new problems exist and that, perhaps, certain theological theses of LALT that have petrified with the passing of years not only do not help in the discussion, but impede it or make it difficult. I am thinking, for example, of all the prejudices against the notions of efficiency and competitiveness that exist in ecclesial environments and popular movements committed to the poor. The attractive proposal of an 'economy of solidarity', organized solely under the principle of solidarity, without relations of competition and, therefore, without the notion of efficiency, feeds the dream that it is possible to build in history a new society, a society that would be a magnification of the communitarian life on the macrosocial scale.[10] As João B. Libânio says, 'up to today *the Christian dream is communitarian*. The idealized community, traced by Luke in the Acts of the Apostles, persists as

---

10 For example, E. Mance, *Revolução das redes*, Petrópolis, Vozes, 2000; and the Campanha da Fraternidade, 1999. For a different vision of those two texts on solidarity and competition in a society of increased solidarity, see: H. Assmann and J. M. Sung, *Competência e sensibilidade solidária: educar para esperança*, Petrópolis, Vozes, 2000, ch. 4.

inspirational model of communities.'[11] And when that dream is seen as or transformed into a concrete social project, there is no more debate over the problem of the efficiency of an economic-social organization or public institution. The lack of debate, in turn, leads to the making of mistaken decisions when the scarcity of time demands a decision.

Beyond the difficulty with the notion of efficiency, we also have a strong prejudice towards all that relates to freedom in and of the market. The option for the poor of the Christian churches of Latin America and of LALT was always taken in the name of a non-capitalist society and, with that, there almost appeared between us an interdict with respect to freedom in and of the market. This is why astonishment and malaise appears when a popular government assumes the banner of free trade at a WTO meeting.

As we saw above, in the citation of Gutiérrez, if LALT wants to remain as a critical reflection it must also assume the task of constantly criticizing its own foundations. Therefore, one must be allowed to ask such questions as: are there any presuppositions and reflections of LALT that have already become almost dogmas that today block the practice and search for meaning more than they illuminate and open new perspectives for action? Might it be that the reflections of LALT, which has been elaborated primarily in a situation where these problems and questions were not faced, are still capable of illuminating the practices and spiritual life of the activists who are confronted with these new social realities?

Re-examining some socio-analytical positions

Continuing our reflection, I want to bring up here the second innovative characteristic of LALT: the use of socio-analytical mediations. The dialectic articulation with praxis, the use of socio-analytical mediations and the notion of the God-of-Life who opts for the poor, and, therefore, the relation between theology and economic, social, political, and ecological aspects that threaten the life of the weakest constitute, without doubt, some of the central elements of what we can call the paradigm of LALT.

The substitution of the social sciences for philosophy as the main interlocutor of theology, and, more than that, the recognition that one

---

11 J. B. Libânio, 'Prospectivas teológicas e pastorais do Cristianismo na América Latina e no Caribe: trajetórias, diagnósticos, prospectivas', in W. L. Sanchez (ed.), *Cristianismo na América Latina e no Caribe*, São Paulo, Paulinas, 2003, p. 328.

cannot do theology today without a theoretical mediation of social sciences constitutes one of the great ruptures of LALT in relation to other theologies of the last century.

As Agnes Heller says, in premodern societies, because of their stratified structure, there was no need for any sociology to explain society.[12] Philosophy and theology, which formulated their truths *sub specie aeternitatis*, were well up to that task. The truths valid for all time and carriers of an eternal message explained immobile societies, and they perceived productive technique as part of nature. With modern societies, which are structured by a division of labour, the relation between the individual and society becomes fluid, and the past, present, and future are transformed into human creations. In a world such as this, philosophy and theology understood as bearing eternal truths are no longer able to explain the functioning of society and the necessity of the social sciences appears.

Thus, the adoption of socio-analytic mediation means the acceptance of the modern world and the fact that modern societies move quickly and that, therefore, certain social theories can be true and useful at one moment and no longer so in another when society will have changed. Seeing this, let us re-examine the subject of the idolatry of the market briefly articulated when we mentioned the defence of the free market by the G-22. Is the G-22 falling into an idolatry of the market? Can a government or groups committed to the cause of the poor accept the logic of the market or negotiate within the rules of the market?

The concept of the idolatry of the market, which came from within LALT, was spread around the world and appears as much in official documents of the Vatican as in the texts of defenders and critics of capitalism. We can say that this concept is one of the great contributions of LALT to Western thought. But, this notion is not always understood in the same way and there are many who identify the critique of the idolatry of the market with the critique of the market. I think that clarifying what is behind that concept a little more can greatly help us in our positions regarding the governments and political and social groups that deal with the global economy and international trade.

Critique of market idolatry in the thought of Hugo Assmann

Hugo Assmann, without a doubt, is one of the Latin American theoreticians who has worked at length with this concept of the idolatry

---

12 A. Heller, 'A sociologia como desfetichização da modernidade', *Novos Estudos Cebrap*, July 1991, no 30, pp. 204–14.

of the market. His work, co-authored with Franz Hinkelammert, *A idolatria do mercado* (*The Idolatry of the Market*), continues to be the work of reference for this subject.[13] I think that a quick look at the evolution of Assmann's thought on the market can help us not only to understand this notion, but also the diverse positions critical of the market that we find today.

With respect to the critique of the market, we can divide Assmann's thought into three main phases. The first one is from the beginning of LALT. In his book *Teología desde la práxis de la liberación* (*Theology From the Praxis of Liberation*), he dialogues with dependency theory and affirms that the concept of liberation is correlated to that of dependency.[14] His use of dependency theory and especially of Marxism is quite critical, to such a point as to affirm that

> for the construction of a socialist society the operationalization of the mythical and symbolic universes is fundamental not only because they exist, as the objective power of the subjective, but also because they correspond to a human social dimension that cannot and must not be suppressed, even when the necessity to articulate them within the historical rationality of humanization is imposed.[15]

However, he shares with the majority of Marxists and socialists of the time the view that in socialist society there is no relevant role for the market. We can deduce this from the fact that he does not say anything, or almost anything, about the market in post-capitalist society. When he deals with the market it is to associate it with capitalist exploitation and the process of fetishization in the capitalist economy. We can say that he makes a metaphysical critique of the market, proposing an economy without the market.

A metaphysical or absolute critique of the market can lead into a proposal for a society based on direct and non-institutional relations, of an anarchist type or a romantic vision of a society functioning as a community, a society 'where freedom reigns': a society where competitive relations would not reign, nor commercial trade, but pure co-operation and solidarity. But, as Assmann had an acute perception of the political and institutional problems of society, his proposal did not go in that direction and thus we can say that in practice socialism was tied to a totally planned economy.

---

13 Assmann and Hinkelammert, *A idolatria do mercado*.

14 H. Assmann, *Teología desde la práxis de la liberación: ensayo teológico desde la América dependiente*, Salamanca, Ed. Sígueme, 1973, pp. 24 and 34.

15 Assmann, *Teología*, p. 194.

In the beginning of the 1980s, Assmann initiated his second phase, deepening his critique of capitalism beginning with the notions of fetishism and idolatry. He says, for example:

> the capitalist mode of production, as Marx tried to show, rests basically on a fetishization process. Capitalism is the social construction of appearances. And this ideological construction is not at all secularized. It is deeply 'religious'. Therefore, recently, an increasing number of liberation theologians have started to say that our theological task is characterized as anti-fetishism and anti-idolatry. The system rests on the strength of its idols.[16]

The apex of this second phase comes with the publication of *The Idolatry of the Market*. In the preface he writes:

> The subjects that we approach more carefully are: the way economic rationality 'kidnapped' and functionalized essential aspects of Christianity: 'economic religion' unleashed a vast process of idolatry, which finds its most evident expression in the supposed self-regulation of market mechanisms; that economic idolatry feeds on a sacrificial ideology that involves constant sacrifices of human lives.[17]

Assmann thus unmasks the idolatry of the market, the market elevated to the category of absolute through the transcendentalizations carried out by liberal and neoliberal economic theory. This critique is not one that is critical of the market in itself, as it was in the first phase, but critical of its absolutization and of the economic religion into which capitalism had transformed. He criticizes not the market itself, but the idolatry of the market. According to him,

> idols are gods of oppression. Biblically, the concept of idol and idolatry was directly linked to the manipulation of religious symbols in order to create subjects, legitimize oppression, and support the ruling powers in the organization of human conviviality. . . . If we speak of idolatry and 'perverse theologies' present in the economy it is because we are concerned about the sacrifice of human lives legitimized by idolatrous conceptions of economic processes.[18]

---

16 H. Assmann, 'A Teologia da Libertação faz caminho ao andar', in [various authors] *Fé cristã e ideologia*, Piracicaba/ S.Bernardo do Campo, Unimep/ Imprensa Metodista, 1981, p. 79.

17 Assmann and Hinkelammert, *A idolatria do mercado*, p. 7.

18 Assmann and Hinkelammert, *A idolatria do mercado*, pp. 11–12.

My insistence on saying that he no longer makes a metaphysical critique of the market, but a critique of the idolatry of the market is due to the fact that many still confuse the two, and, therefore, would not do anything 'in accord' with the market because this would be to fall into idolatry.

This change of Assmann's position is due, among other factors, to the assimilation of Franz Hinkelammert's thesis that utopias (like the total market, perfect planning, or a society without institutions and laws) are horizons necessary for giving meaning to historical projects, but impossible to realize in history.[19] Even more, any attempt to realize fully a utopia, that is, any attempt to identify an historical project with a utopia, ends up leading to a demand for human sacrifices. Therefore, Assmann says that

> totalizing economic paradigms – only market, only planning – try to direct exclusive and unique paths, legitimated with messianic promises. . . . the claim to exclusivity and universal validity is made through the elimination of obstacles along the road, declaring it the only passable road, transforming it into a necessary operation. The cost in human lives is transformed into necessary sacrifices.[20]

The deepening of the theories of fetishism and idolatry and the assimilation of the critique of utopian reason made by Hinkelammert are new theoretical features that push Assmann to overcome (not in the metaphysical sense, but in the dialectical sense of overcoming) dependency theory and to arrive at a more complex socio-analytical vision that allows him to elaborate one of his more important contributions in the area of the theology.

For us to understand well what occurs in the shift from the second to the third phase, we need to return to the phrase already cited from the preface of *The Idolatry of the Market*: '"economic religion" unleashed a vast process of idolatry, which finds its most evident expression in the supposed self-regulation of market mechanisms.' At the end of the 1980s, Assmann identified two sources of market idolatry: the requirement of sacrifices of human lives and the claim of the supposed self-regulation of market mechanisms. However, in a later text he will reformulate this critique of the self-regulation of the market.

Assmann, who since the beginning of the 1980s has taught in the postgraduate programme in education at the Methodist University

---

19 F. Hinkelammert, *Crítica a la razón utópica*, San José (Costa Rica), DEI, 1984.

20 Assmann and Hinkelammert, *A idolatria do mercado*, pp. 291–2.

of Piracicaba, started to dialogue more with the natural sciences, especially with new theories in the area of the mathematics, such as chaos theory, physics, chemistry, biology, and neuroscience. Without abandoning his lessons from the social and human sciences, he incorporated in his reflection other areas of knowledge and other themes, such as self-organization and self-regulation, the emergence of new properties, autopoiesis, theories of cognition, etc. Thus, a few years after the critique of the claim of market self-regulation, he wrote:

Self-regulation or *self-organization* is a key concept, today, in all scientific fields where auto-(re)generative processes are discussed, in other words, programmes that (re)programme themselves and that contain relatively autonomous levels. . . . Self-regulation is the notion with which one claims to explain the supposed or real internal circular causality of spontaneous orders. Internal mechanisms automatically regulate the system's functioning. The key for the rational explanation of the internal phenomena must be sought within the internal mechanisms themselves. It is the case of living organisms. . . .

The crucial question, therefore, is not in admitting that the market has self-regulating mechanisms, but in knowing up to what point they are inclusive and/or exclusive.[21]

This text can be considered one of the representative texts beginning his third phase in the critique of the market. The critique now no longer concerns the claim of self-regulation, which he already admits, but the excluding character of this self-regulating mechanism. Behind the application of the theory of self-regulation in social sciences is a question concerning how it is possible that societies so ample and complex as the current ones function. In the past the central enquiry of the social sciences was to understand how societies function in order to be able to transform them or maintain them. The search for understanding how society functions presupposed the fact of a society that functions and reproduces itself. The new question concerns that presupposition: how is it possible that the fragmented actions of so many people and social groups create a certain social order that reproduces itself without a centralized command? We are not going to enter into that discussion here, but it is important to point out that the third phase of Assmann's thought on the market is born of his dialogue with

---

21 H. Assmann, *Desafios e falácias: ensaios sobre a conjuntura atual*, São Paulo, Paulinas, 1991, pp. 23–4.

natural sciences and social sciences and philosophies that work in a transdisciplinary way with these concepts.[22]

That new dialogue led Assmann to a position that for many supporters of LALT became incomprehensible:

> Among the undeniable things, in the area of human interactions in complex societies, is the existence and functionality of partially self-regulating dynamic systems, in which one refers to human behaviours. In the economy, this question has a name, which was rejected by many sectors of the left until today: the market. Do we know how to join social consciousness and the ethical subject with the (partial) self-regulation of the market?

> *To accept, critically but positively, the market*, without giving up the goals of solidarity, demands a new reflection on the very concept of the ethical subject, individual and collective. . . . It is a question of considering jointly individual ethical options and the objectification, material and institutional, of values, under the form of normatization of human conviviality with strong self-regulating connotations.[23]

Thus Assmann began by criticizing the market in an absolute way and later moved toward the critique of the idolatry of the market, arriving at a critical but positive acceptance of the market, without giving up the goals of solidarity. Moreover, he affirms that the ethics of solidarity itself needs to be incarnate in normatizations of human conviviality with self-regulating connotations, that is, the social goals and practices of solidarity must not be restricted to conscientious and intentional actions, but institutional mechanisms of solidarity that function in a self-regulating way must be created. It is the overcoming of a merely voluntarist and conscientious vision of solidarity and social goals to incorporate self-regulating institutional mechanisms. (It is important for us to understand in this notion the difference between the visions of Assmann and Capra, which we will see further below.)

The recognition by Assmann of the fact that there exist self-regulating mechanisms in societies and that the market is one of these does not mean the abandonment on his part of the critique of the idolatry of the market. Now the critique of the idolatry of the market is founded on two pillars: the belief, on the part of the neoliberals, that

---

22 H. Assmann, *Reencantar a educação*, Petrópolis, Vozes, 1998. He presents in the second part a most interesting glossary on those new concepts.

23 H. Assmann, *Metáforas novas para reencantar a educação*, Piracicaba, Unimep, 1996, p. 64. (Emphasis mine.)

the self-organization of the market will always produce the best result, that is, faith in the always beneficial character of the self-organization of the market that hinders any social intervention in view of social goals; and the sacrificialism that results from this belief, that is, the sacrifices of human lives demanded and realized by an economic system that is presented as without alternative and as the only way to realize social solidarity.[24]

I think that the new features in the area of social reality – like the sprouting of the information society, economic globalization, the destruction of the socialist bloc, and the few results in view of the independent effort of education and popular pastorals centred on the notions of conscientization and the historical subject – and the constant revision of 'socio-analytical mediations' led Assmann constantly to review his theoretical positions, until arriving at the affirmation that 'the market is a complex interpenetration of tendencies of exclusion and inclusion, and excluding trends prevail where public policies related to social goals are lacking'.[25]

These revisions, however, do not signify change in his radical option for the defence of the life of the poor and the victims of history. They mean only that for theology to remain self-critical it must rethink constantly its historical foundations and mediations, its projects, and its images of God. So as Assmann himself says, 'the relation – which does not stop being a very demanding dialectical tension between the utopian horizon and historical projects – compels us to take seriously the Biblical prohibition against possessing definitive images of God,' and also – I add – definitive conceptions of social projects or of critiques of capitalism.[26]

To maintain faith in a God who is revealed both in the face of the poor and the victim and in sharing with others the pleasures of life, and at the same time to rethink the categories of our social and economic analysis is a difficult challenge. Nonetheless, it is necessary for a theology or a social theory that considers itself to be at the service of social, political, and religious practices that will favour the poor and the victims. The metaphysical critique of capitalism or the market system and the intransigent defence of voluntarist and idealistic social

---

24 The basic difference between liberation theologians, like Assmann, Hinkelammert, and J. Santa Ana, who work with the notion of sacrifice, and scholars of the role of sacrifice in religion and society, like Girard, is that the latter study sacrifices carried through by priests, while the former analyse sacrifices demanded and carried through by social and economic structures and systems.

25 H. Assmann, 'Por uma teologia humanamente saudável', in Susin (ed.), O mar se abriu, p. 124.

26 Assmann and Hinkelammert, A idolatria do mercado, p. 420.

projects can feed the self-esteem of those who consider themselves prophets of the new world, but cannot help in the concrete decisions that must be made within the popular struggles and organizations or in the negotiations of international trade.

Capra and economic self-organization

The use in social sciences of concepts like self-organization, self-regulation, and the emergence of new properties and new orders is increasing, and even diverse liberal and neoliberal authors are using these concepts to legitimize the currently dominant global economic model. As I have already dealt with this subject in another text, I will briefly analyse one other anti-capitalist author who uses these concepts in order to see the differences with Assmann's analysis.[27]

Fritjof Capra, a well-known thinker and follower of the theory of complex systems or complexity paradigm, says that a basic characteristic of life is

the spontaneous emergence of a new order. That phenomenon occurs in critical moments of instability provoked by fluctuations of the environment and enhanced by feedback links. The spontaneous emergence results in the creation of things that are, many times, qualitatively different from the phenomena from which they appeared. The constant generation of new features – the 'creative advance of nature,' in the words of philosopher Alfred North Whitehead – is a basic property of all living systems.[28]

This notion of the spontaneous emergence of a new order, that is, of an order qualitatively distinct from the previous one that appears without having been previously planned nor executed by a subject external to the living system itself is one of the foundations of the new theories of life sciences and complex systems. When Assmann writes about the self-regulating or self-organizing mechanism of the market system he is referring to that logic. Not all authors who work with this notion in the fields of chemistry and biology accept its use in the fields of social and human sciences, but Capra – like Assmann, Niklas

---

27 J. M. Sung, *Sujeito e sociedades complexas: para repensar os horizontes utópicos*, Petrópolis, Vozes, 2002, ch. 4, 'Nova forma de legitimação da economia' ('The New Form of Legitimation of the Economy').

28 F. Capra, *As conexões ocultas: ciência para uma vida sustentável*, São Paulo, Cultrix, 2002, p. 127. [English language edn: *The Hidden Connections: A Science for Sustainable Living*, Glasgow, HarperCollins, 2002.]

Luhman, Paul Krugman, and many other authors – thinks that it can also be applied to the understanding of the social order and says that in a human organization 'the new order is not invented by any individual in particular, but appears spontaneously as a result of the collective creativity of the organization'.[29]

The fact of recognizing the emergence of new properties and, with this, the sprouting of a new order by the interaction and feedback of the elements pertaining to a system and between these elements and the system itself is not to say that human organizations are totally unconscious or devoid of any type of conscientiously projected structures. For Capra,

> human organizations always contain projected structures and emergent structures. The projected or planned structures are the formal structures of organization, which consist of official documents. Emergent structures are created by the informal nets of the organization and by communities of practice. The two types of structures are, as already we saw, very different, and all organizations need both.[30]

However, when Capra deals with the globalization process, that is, the sprouting of a new world-wide order of a magnitude and complexity never before seen, he leaves aside the notion of the spontaneous emergence of new orders and says that

> the process of economic globalization was elaborated intentionally by the great capitalist countries (the so-called 'G-7'), the principle multinational companies and global financial institutions – among which are distinguished the World Bank, International Monetary Fund (IMF), and the World Trade Organization (WTO) – were created expressly towards that end.[31]

This emphasis on the intentionality behind the process of economic globalization raises the following question: why does he set the theory of the spontaneous, non-intentional, emergence of new orders in complex systems in the background and place all the focus on intentionality? This is a central question to the extent that he says that economic globalization is the deeper root of the 'majority of our present environmental and social problems', thus demanding a deeper systemic change.[32]

---

29 Capra, *As conexões ocultas*, p. 128.
30 Capra, *As conexões ocultas*, p. 132.
31 Capra, *As conexões ocultas*, p. 150.
32 Capra, *As conexões ocultas*, p. 220.

The indication for this theoretical 'slip' – that slip from the emphasis on spontaneous emergence to the intentional and directed production of globalization – is his certainty that the change is already occurring under the direction of coalitions formed by academics, leaders, and activists from around the world. One can only think that this change is being considered and directed in an intentional way if one assumes that the globalization process was also imposed and directed in an intentional way. Therefore, he says:

> Any realistic discussion about this turn [systemic change] must begin with the fact that, though globalization is an emergent phenomenon, the current form of economic globalization was conscientiously projected and *it can* be modified. . . . The 'global market' is, in reality, a web of machines – an automaton that imposes its logic on all the human participants. However, to function without hard jolts, this automaton must be programmed by people and human institutions.[33]

Capra returns to the idea of the emergence of new orders that was absent in his previous affirmation concerning the origin of the globalization process, but, contrary to the theory previously accepted concerning spontaneous emergence, he places it in the background. All the emphasis is placed on the thesis that globalization was intentionally and conscientiously projected. However, this idea about the modification process of globalization is not in accordance with the theory he previously accepted in which the modification of complex orders is not totally controllable or subject to conscientious planning. In accordance with the theory of complex systems, one can plan and try to control, but complex systems always react in unforeseen ways, generating unintended effects and, in situations of high instability, causing the emergence of a new self-organizing and autopoietic order. That is, we can intervene with changes, but we cannot control them fully. This vision of autopoiesis is one of the ruptures with the mechanist paradigm realized through the systemic and organic vision of living systems.

However, Capra, one of the first great critics of the mechanist vision of the world, returns to the machine metaphor, the global market as a web of machines, in order to ground his proposal of the new social order. He wants to show that the process of economic globalization can be created and modified and, not only that, be created and modified in a way that functions 'without hard jolts', needing for that to

---

33 Capra, *As conexões ocultas*, p. 221.

be programmed by people and human institutions. He believes that the current globalization was intentionally planned and executed and also believes that a new globalization, with an ecologically sustainable economy, can be planned and executed. More than that, he affirms that the objective conditions for this already exist, lacking only the political will and priorities: 'the numerous ecological projects of which we spoke in the preceding pages make it clear that the transition towards a sustainable future already is not a technical or conceptual problem, but a problem of values and political will.'[34]

Everything would be a question of political will and values that we can accept conscientiously. There would be no emergence of orders, nor scarcity of technical knowledge, not only of what occurs in the world today, but also of all the effects of our actions and the reactions of the global system and the ecological system to our actions. Also, there would not be a scarcity of materials and desired objects,[35] nor scarcity of the sensibility of solidarity and ethical experience that make people and groups set their desires and interests aside on behalf of the common good. And all that without speaking of the difficulty of all humanity coming to an agreement on what constitutes the common good.

That line of thought leads people to believe that political will and new human values are enough to break with the current economic globalization or to keep ourselves totally outside of commercial agreements like those discussed in the WTO or in the negotiations in view of the FTAA.[36] Everything would be a question of the will of 'popular' governments and the directors of social organizations, such as co-operatives.

With these reflections and questions I do not want to say that multilateral institutions like the IMF, WTO, BIS, WB, the countries of the G-7, and large transnational companies do not have enormous power in the global economy.[37] It is one thing to say that they occupy privi-

---

34 Capra, *As conexões ocultas*, p. 264.

35 Desired objects are scarce by definition, as non-scarce goods are not desired objects. The scarcity of desired objects in relation to the desires of people is one of the reasons for human conflicts. This theme was treated in chapters 2 and 3 of this volume.

36 Translator's note: The FTAA – *Free Trade Area of the Americas* – is an agreement established in 1994 among 34 countries under which all participating countries, through regular negotiations, are to work towards regional integration and free trade. For more information visit http://www.ftaa-alca.org/alca_e.asp.

37 Translator's note: BIS, *Bank for International Settlements*; WB, World Bank.

leged places within the system and possess much power, but another thing to say that the system as a whole was created and is being directed by them. That would be to place them outside the system, like a transcendental subject. That is not the truth. Moreover, if they acted as one cohesive unit and really had all that power, there would be no crises among the enormous companies, like Enron, nor would there be a systemic crisis of capitalism.

Capitalism passes through cyclical systemic crises precisely because, as a complex system, it is not planned and directed by any suprasystemic entity. It is because of those cyclical crises of the capitalist system that we can think about the transformations within capitalism itself and about moving beyond the capitalist system towards another economic and social system. However, the systemic character of the crisis itself shows us that the possible surpassing or changing of paths can be influenced, but not totally directed towards an intentionally pre-established path. This would require a transcendental subject, who is outside the system/history and with full knowledge and omnipotence to foresee and annul all the unintended effects of all the members and elements of the system: an image of a god functionary to our desires, an idol.

Anthropology and original sin

We can see that Capra is much more optimistic than Assmann in relation to our capacities for scientific knowledge, the human disposition for a holy life or, in the language of ecologists, a 'sustainable life' (people who give up their personal desires and interests on behalf of the common good of billions of unknown people). Capra is much more optimistic than Assmann in relation to our capacity to control the evolution of systems as complex as economic globalization and all the conflicts that arise from the inevitable internal contradictions in a social order so large and complex, with so much cultural, religious, and social diversity.

I think that his optimism in relation to our abilities is born of his desire, which is often transformed into certainty, that this new sustainable order without scarcity and conflicts is possible.[38] Since for that it

---

38 Capra and other ecologists think of scarcity in relation to basic necessities and, with that, the world already would no longer live in a state of scarcity as the total product of the world is greater than the basic necessities of humanity. However, the concept of scarcity in the present economy and also in this article is in relation to desires, as what moves people are fundamentally desires. For the relation between necessities and desires, see Chapter 2 of this volume.

is necessary to move beyond all of our limits in facing the large and complex human and social orders, he ends up, basically, denying the human condition with its limits and contradictions or believing that in the future, with the evolution of the human being, we will surpass it.[39]

Assmann, in turn, affirms that human beings do not tend naturally to be in solidarity with others, as we assume in our dreams of a just and fraternal society. Yet they are not only egoistic and inimical to solidarity, as the underlying anthropology of neoliberalism assumes. We are ambiguous beings with tendencies towards egoism and the potential for solidarity. Avoiding those two extremes, he intends to recoup the wise and realistic side of the myths of the fall or corruption. Therefore, Assmann affirms that 'the question of original sin is a kind of interpretive key concerning what one can expect from human beings in communal life'.[40]

Kingdom of God, community, and popular organization

In the face of a social reality so large and complex as economic globalization, if we think of the struggle for the Kingdom of God as a struggle for a society exempt from poverty, injustice, oppression, and domination and full of freedom and fraternity, there will be nothing but frustration and relief of the type 'we had hoped . . .' It is clear that we must desire such a society, but we must also know that this image of the Kingdom of God within history is only a horizon that gives meaning to our lives and struggles, but is not and could never be a historical project of the society to be constructed.

Our struggles for a more just society generate reactions from groups that do not want to lose their privileges as well as unintended effects that will generate new problems and new challenges. It is in this way that human societies evolve, modifying and maintaining themselves. Totally stable systems are dead systems. Living systems, composites of living and not-living beings (such as persons, institutions and material goods), remain alive because of the constant tension with disorder and disequilibrium.

However, many of us were formed in a theology that preached the struggle for *the construction of the Kingdom of God*, as if it were

---

39 Edgar Morin, another well-known name in this area, is much less optimistic and works from the 'human condition' and, therefore, believes that this new order without conflicts and crises is impossible. See, for example, E. Morin, *Método 5: a humanidade da humanidade*, Porto Alegre, Sulina, 2002.

40 Assmann, *Reencantar a educação*, p. 20.

a human work that could be fully realized (the construction would one day end) within history such that the ambiguities and relations of domination and injustice would not fit within it. It is a world or a state beyond human possibilities, which is the reason it is called the Kingdom of God. The contradiction is that this Kingdom was seen as the fruit of human action, of conscientious and organized people.

In the face of the impasses and frustrations of struggling to construct within human history a Kingdom that, through its characteristics, is beyond the human condition, many abandoned or left in second or third place the political, social, and economic challenges that resulted from globalization and the technological revolution. They turned more to practices in the micro-social field, trying to construct in the community environment what cannot obtain on the macro-social scale.

There are also those who try to overcome this impasse by directing their critiques at the concept of the Kingdom of God itself and propose the notion of reign of God. Antonio González, for example, criticizes the conception of the Kingdom of God where the Trinity would represent for us a model of the relation between human beings in a society free of poverty, injustice, inequality and violence and where abundance and fraternity would reign. For him, in this perspective the 'Trinity acquires an old function of the deity in classical philosophy. It is the Immovable Mover that attracts to itself all things, moved in last instance by the desire to be like it.'[41] He also criticizes the tendency to emphasize our ethical obligation to construct the Kingdom in accordance with the model of the Trinity.

Moreover, he emphasizes that, 'from the point of view of the poor, this conception of the relation between the Trinity and the Kingdom of God is not especially hopeful. The poor are less enabled to transform history than other more powerful subjects, from the way that their function tends to become secondary.'[42]

From these quite reasonable critiques, he proposes the notion of the trinitarian reign of God. The reign is seen in the first place as a dynamism already present in history and not a state of things still being constructed. According to González there are two areas in this dynamism: first, 'aspects and dimensions of the world that, in fact, oppose the reign of God, and over which, in fact, God still cannot reign. They are the economic, political, social, or religious powers that oppose the designs of God for history, and that therefore are responsible in the

41 A. González, 'El reinado trinitario del Dios Cristiano', in [various authors], *A esperança dos pobres vive: coletânea em homenagem aos 80 anos de José Comblin*, São Paulo, Paulus, 2003, pp. 460.

42 González, 'El reinado', p. 461.

end for injustice, suffering, and oppression'; and second, 'the areas of creation over which God can exercise God's reign. And that means, very concretely, that in them any form of domination of some human beings over others disappears, because where God in fact already reigns there are no other kings or masters.'[43]

He thus divides the world into two distinct spaces: the sphere of the economic, political, social, and religious powers responsible for the suffering and oppression in the world, where God does not reign; and a second sphere where God does reign and, therefore, where all forms of domination disappear. But, where is this wonderful world without any forms of domination? For González, this world is the sphere of community:

> [T]he reign of God creates from now on and from below reconciled communities of brothers and sisters, in which already there is no inequality, poverty, or domination. In which, more radically, the fear of God, the insatiable anguish to possess, and the radical serpentine claim of justifying ourselves by the results of our own practice disappear. . . . This reign is not a spiritual entity, but rather a reality in history. God reigns where, through faith, there disappears the consequences of the sin of Adam and appears a reconciled community in which goods are shared, social differences disappear, and poverty is overcome.[44]

In this passage the author presents two dimensions of the reign of God in the community. The first occurs on the personal-subjective level: the people are free of the fear of God, the insatiable anxiety to possess, and the pretension to justify their existence by the results of their practice. That is, the subjective aspect of the liberation of God's reign would consist in the overcoming of a sadistic and sacrificial vision of God by encountering the God of mercy; in the overcoming of consumerism and the desire to feel superior to the other through the greater ownership of goods by discovering that it is in the fraternal encounter with the other that we realize ourselves as persons; and, finally, in the overcoming of the always present temptation of justification and salvation through one's own self-sufficient works by encountering the grace of God that saves us.

The second occurs in the more objective field: the creation of a historical reality, a community, where there is no more social inequal-

---

43 González, 'El reinado', p. 463.
44 González, 'El reinado', pp. 463 and 467.

ity and poverty, but sharing. It is the objective aspect of the liberation and reign of God. It is clear that the author, like Libânio in the text quoted above, is inspired by the ideal model of community presented in the book of Acts 4.32–35.

I do not want to discuss here up to what point that ideal community was realized by the first Christian communities; first, because I am not an exegete, and second, because our reality is very different. But we cannot forget, referring to that community as a community where the reign of God lives, that even in the book of Acts the problems with that model are made clear. First we have the example of Ananias and Sapphira (Acts 5.1–11), which shows that this beautiful intention was not fully accepted by all. Later there was the problem of the Hellenists complaining about the way the administrators of the common good dealt with the scarcity of goods by neglecting their widows in favour of the Hebrew widows (Acts 6.1). Later there was the famine that overtook the community of Jerusalem when there was nothing more to share. The problem of scarcity is always confounding our good intentions and beautiful desires.

I brought this article by González into the debate because he presents in a quite interesting manner an attempt to find a way through the impasse in place since the beginning of this chapter: between a) the concept of liberation and the notion of the Kingdom of God, and b) the reality of scarcity. At first sight the solution presented by González seems to be quite interesting, especially in the subjective dimension of encountering the God of mercy and the experience of grace. We can say that it is the experience of liberation, the experience of becoming free, in the very going down the path of the struggle for liberation. But, in presenting the community in the terms set by him as the location of the event of God's reign today, his proposal does not illuminate or help the concrete struggle of communities.

Except for some small communities that are completely isolated from the modern world and certain types of religious communities, it is no longer possible to live in communities where one can practice sharing and overcome social inequality and poverty. Contemporary society no longer functions as small ancient communities. People live with their families and work, either in rural or urban areas, and live off the fruits of work in the form of wages or income. People can share the various wages and incomes within their families, but this sharing does not occur and nobody feels called or obligated to do it within their local or ecclesial community.

When a person or a group experiences in community the mercy and grace of God and assumes the cause of the life of the poor, those people and groups do not participate in the communities described by González, but in movements or associations of political and social struggles or they participate in some NGO or type of co-operative that seeks to increase the income and consumption capacity of the poor and the quality of their lives. So that the experience of grace, the reign of God in personal life, becomes historical, the next step is to enter into an organization. And in organizations concrete and difficult situations arise like the one caused by the director of the co-operative mentioned earlier.

A popular organization – whether a union, school, NGO, co-operative, or tenants' association – and a community are not identical things. If they were, we would not use different names to refer to them. And the necessity of different names discloses that an organization has characteristics and functional logics different from those of a community.

According to Peter Drucker,

> in contrast to communities, societies, or families, organizations are intentionally conceived and always specialized. Communities and societies are defined by the ties that bind its members, be they language, culture, history, or locality. An organization is defined by its task. A symphony orchestra does not try to cure the sick; it plays music. The hospital takes care of the sick people, but it does not try to play Beethoven.[45]

And to the extent that an organization is a tool defined by its specific objective, we have the problem of efficiency. An organization that does not reach its specific objective has no reason to exist and probably will not last long. And it is not enough to reach its objectives, as it must reach them with an efficient use of its scarce resources. An aid agency, for example, that it is not efficient – that is, one that does not manage well its human resources, finances, time, and equipment – can survive so long as it can finance its inefficiency and the members of that agency will keep their jobs as long as that source lasts. However, the population assisted is greatly harmed by the bad service and a part of its potential public who could be taken care of is not.

Let us come back to the case of the impasse in that co-operative facing the necessity of deciding whether or not to fire an inefficient director. It was the experience of the mercy of God, the experience

---

45 P. Drucker, *Administrando em tempos de grandes mudanças*, São Paulo, Pioneira, 1999, p. 64.

of not feeling guilty in the face of overwhelming situations, and feeling called to join with the community to seek a life worthy for the collectivity, that led the group to create a co-operative. And in the co-operative they had perceived that one cannot realize the objective of improving income and the consumption of the local population only with the criteria of reconciliation and solidarity; they perceived that they also need to be efficient and competitive in the market. If God's reign occurs in communities based on the single principle of solidarity, sharing and lacking social inequality, the reign of God would be absent not only in economic globalization or the struggle of the G-22, but also in this co-operative if the decision makers privilege the survival of the co-operative and fire the inefficient director. And if that is true, the Christians who desire to live under the reign of God must not leave the sphere of the community to enter into any type of social or popular organization, much less to assume ranks in the machine of the state; even if to struggle for liberation or a better life for all. That would be in contradiction with the proposal itself to struggle for a more just society in name of the God of life.

I think that this paradox or contradiction helps us understand many of the current difficulties of communication between Christians who keep solely to the sphere of the community or in merely demanding or contestatory movements and those people originating from communities that had assumed functions in state or non-state organizations in order to respond to new challenges and opportunities emerging within social and political practices in favour of the poor and the victims. There is not only a communication difficulty, but also a sensation that many of the theological discussions of LALT no longer help these activists find a deeper meaning for their practices within the contradictions and limits of organizations and economic globalization.

Final words

All those paradoxes – as much in the struggles on the level of international trade and globalization, as in popular organizations – show that there is something very problematic in our theologies. Struggling for the liberalization of the market does not always mean falling into the arms of neoliberalism or into the idolatry of the market, as the use of the criterion of efficiency in organizations like unions, associations, and co-operatives does not necessarily mean abandoning the criteria of the reign of God. As also, the mere preaching of the reign of God does not necessarily mean participating in the concrete struggles of the poor.

Will the group of theologians who still claim to produce theologies committed to the causes of the poor and the victims of history be capable of sufficient creativity to rethink the foundations of LALT beginning with our challenges and new questions that come from praxis? Will we be able to continue elaborating theological reflections that feed the faith of the people committed to the cause of the poor and the victims within the contradictions, limits, and scarcity of our social world? I think yes! For this we need to pay more attention to the voices that come from praxis, re-evaluate the theoretical mediations that we have used, consciously or unconsciously, and dialogue constantly with the new theories of social, human, and natural sciences. Only by returning constantly to our 'socio-analytical mediations' and hermeneutics can we as a theological community continue giving our theological, faithful service to the God of the poor, the weak, and the victims who is revealed to us within the practice of liberation.

After recognizing that because of the human condition it is impossible to construct within history the reign or Kingdom of God in its fullness and that, therefore, liberation will not arrive in the form it was and continues to be dreamed, does the term 'liberation' in Liberation Theology still make sense? And if we abandon the idea of liberation, what happens to the meaning of the announcement that 'it is for freedom that Christ freed us' (Gal. 5.1)? Is liberation a point of arrival after a long struggle for the construction of the Kingdom of God, or does the experience of liberation come within the struggle itself for the liberation of the poor? Is liberation the freedom that we experience in the commitment to the struggle itself, in the experience itself of encountering Christ and knowing him in encountering the poor? What is the relation between the struggle for the liberation of the poor, which is impossible in its fullness, with Christian freedom?[46] These are serious questions for which I do not have the condition or the pretension to respond now.

But, so as not to finish this chapter with a series of questions, I want to appeal to a quote from Father Comblin. He says that

Latin American Liberation Theology, to be able to continue and to save itself from the destiny of temporary phenomena, must integrate itself into the great current that derives from the New Testament's message of freedom, which traverses all Christianity, even if often marginalized, and affirms its strength in the Reformation. This

---

46 On this relation, see, for example, J. Konings, 'A verdade vos tornará livres' in [various authors], *A esperança dos pobres vive*, pp. 167–73.

current of freedom is one of the sources of modernity, is confronted with modernity, and dialogues with this modernity up to the present day.

And that

the greater reproach that one can direct to liberation theology is for not having dedicated enough attention to the true drama of the human person, to its destination, vocation, and, consequently, to the depths of the question of freedom.[47]

---

[47] J. Comblin, *Cristãos rumo ao século XXI: nova caminhada de libertação*, São Paulo, Paulus, 1996, pp. 117 and 344.

6

Liberation Christianity: A Failed Utopia?

In the 1970s the world saw the birth in Latin America of a new kind of Christianity which would influence not only Western Christian societies but also groups on other continents and of other religions. This movement, which reached its zenith in the 1980s and began to decline in the 1990s, is considered by many to belong to the past. At the same time others consider it very much alive and almost as vigorous as it was before. However, in treating social phenomena of this magnitude which are contemporary with our own generation, we must be cautious about judgements that are as definitive as these.

In this discussion certain questions are always present to the debaters, among them: Did Latin American Christianity or Liberation Theology fail to make its utopia a reality? That is the theme of the present chapter.

Before entering into the discussion itself I wish to make it clear that I will not speak of Latin American Christianity in its entirety, since not every sector of Christianity has struggled for a utopia or for the project of a post-capitalist society and are accordingly going through a certain sense of failure or disenchantment caused by the non-realization of this utopia – often called 'the building of the Kingdom of God' – but I will speak of a minority within Latin American Christianity which Michael Löwy called 'Liberation Christianity'.[1]

Liberation Christianity is an ample social and religious movement with a new religious culture that expresses the socio-historical conditions marked by subordination to the international capitalist system – today global – mass poverty, institutionalized violence, and popular religiosity. Many call it 'Liberation Theology', but since the movement arose before the theology did and the majority of its activists are

---

1 Michael Löwy, *A guerra dos deuses: Religião e política na América Latina*, Petrópolis, Vozes, 2000, pp. 53–4 and p. 57. [English language edn: *The War of Gods: Religion and Politics in Latin America*, London, Verso, 1996.]

not theologians, this is not the most appropriate term. But today even many theologians who consider themselves part of this movement in the broader sense do not define themselves as Liberation Theologians. Furthermore, another term in use, 'the Church of the poor', is also not the best because this social network extends beyond the institutional limits of the Church. The concept of 'Liberation Christianity', being broader than 'theology' or 'the Church', and including both religious culture and the social network, seems to us to be the most appropriate one to use in treating a certain frustration which has settled in after decades of social and ecclesiastical struggles in the expectation of 'building the Kingdom of God' or in the realization of utopia.

Certainly there are differing historical approaches to the experience of Liberation Christianity in recent decades. I am not going to make a division into historical periods, nor will I analyse the changes that have taken place in ecclesial institutions (whether in the 'official Church' or in the base communities); but I will attempt to offer reflections based on the personal witness and reflection of one who has lived intensely with the 'option for the poor' – Nenuca, a religious woman whom I had the honour to know personally with her community in her 'convent', two rooms in a tenement house (cortiço) in the São Paulo neighbourhood of Brás, in the mid-1970s.

This will not be a biography, nor will it be a recuperation of the memory of this struggle, but a starting point from which I wish to discuss certain crises or problems in the experience of Liberation Christianity in Latin America and, based on this, attempt to discern ways of overcoming some of the theoretical-existential impasses which many of us are living through.

The principal reason for this choice is linked to the understanding that it is a 'religious phenomenon'. The impact of Liberation Christianity in Latin America was not owing, fundamentally, to the institutional structure of the ecclesial base communities (CEBs) or to the theoretical-theological novelty of Liberation Theology or even to new rites – without denying the importance of these factors – but to the life testimony of persons who expressed their religious or spiritual experience in the social or political arena, as 'meeting Jesus in the poor or oppressed person'. That is, we cannot understand Christianity or another religion concretely lived in a particular historical context without taking into consideration the religious-spiritual experience which is the driving force behind it and which gives it meaning. Liberation Theologians themselves insisted much on the fact that Liberation Theology was the second moment, the moment of reflection on the praxis of liberation of the poor, which was the first moment. The 'zero' moment would be the spiritual experience of encountering the person of Jesus in the face of the poor.[2]

This type of approach can be described as the study of 'a point on the hologram',[3] a point, a life, which carries with it the elements and the information that compose the system/ totality in which it is located. It is to seek to understand a given moment or historical period based on the memory and the life of one person.

Faith experience questions theology

Carlos Mesters, in the introduction to the book *Quantas vidas eu tivesse, tantas vidas eu daria!*[4] (*As Many Lives as I Had, As Many Lives Would I Give!*), which Nenuca wrote drawing on her memories, says:

> The portrait of Nenuca which appears in these writings is even so: She never appears alone! From the beginning to the end, from 1953 through 1984, Nenuca presents herself in the midst of the poor, the workers, the abandoned children, the marginalized street people, the prostitutes, forever surrounded by the sisters and companions of the Oblates of St. Benedict. What is impressive in all this is that Nenuca, even at the height of her illness, shortly before her death, never thought of herself *per se* but only thought of herself with a concern for better serving God and the poor.
>
> God and the poor! The train of Nenuca's life always ran on these two rails: God and the poor![5]

Nenuca dedicated herself to the poor, beginning her work in Uruguay and continuing in Brazil for a period that runs from the time

---

2 Gutiérrez says in his book *Teologia da Libertação*: 'Social praxis is converted in the same field where the Christian is playing out – with others – his destiny as a human being and his faith in the Lord of history. Participation in the liberation process is a placement which is obligatory and privileged for real reflection and Christian lives. In them nuances of the word of God are heard which are imperceptible in other existential situations and without which there is not, in the present time, any authentic and fecund fidelity to the Lord.' Gustavo Gutiérrez, *Teologia da Libertação: Perspectivas*, 6th edn, Petrópolis, Vozes, 1986, p. 53. [English language edn: *A Theology of Liberation*, Maryknoll, NY, 1973.]

3 For example, Edgar Morin, *Um ponto no holograma: a história de Vidal, meu pai*, São Paulo, Girafa, 2006.

4 G. Castelvecchi (Nenuca), *Quantas vidas eu tivesse, tantas vidas eu daria!*, São Paulo, Paulinas, 1985.

5 Castelvecchi, *Quantas vidas*, p. 5.

before Vatican II up through the height of Liberation Theology. That is, she lived through three distinct times for the Catholic Church in Latin America: 1) the pre-Conciliar Catholic Church; 2) the period between Vatican II and the rise of the ecclesial base communities and of Liberation Theology; and 3) the beginning of the strongest period of the CEBs and of Liberation Theology.

The book, written at the request of her companions during her illness – cancer – which kept her bedridden and ended with her death, tells her memories of her life and her community. About this act of writing her memories, she says:

> To remember the history of a group, and especially of a religious group, in my case the Oblates [which she had helped to found] is to formulate not only the ideal that brought us together but also to re-live the difficulties of being faithful to the first Love.[6]

The words which follow can give us an idea about the ideal which united her group and impelled her life, the ideal which enabled them to overcome difficulties and continue faithful to this 'first Love':

> 'I came that all might have life.' They are words of Jesus: he came to humans so that all might have abundant life, came to bring full life and free from death. *We who feel called to follow him have nothing else to do.* Like Him, we have to go to human beings, those most deeply immersed in the darkness of death, to announce to them the Sun of Life. Announce to them that God fulfils his promises to free the blind, the lame, the prisoners, the oppressed, and that they will be able to see this Salvation with their own eyes. It was this that the aged Simeon sang, with Jesus in his arms![7]

Her memory and her reminiscence are marked by this ideal and the difficulties of staying faithful to it. Michel de Certeau, in saying that the personality of one who is consecrated to the religious life has 'the worth of an enigma, more than that of an example', asks himself: 'Who is this enigmatic person?' and answers:

> There is no answer except the one that comes from an internal necessity. Because the religious life does not receive its justification from outside. It does not have social utility because there is nothing conformist about it, as though one had to be well 'adapted', fusing one-

---

6 Castelvecchi, *Quantas vidas*, p. 9.
7 Castelvecchi, *Quantas vidas*, p. 142.

self with the wall. Nor is it the simple consequence of a doctrine. What defines it is not the benefit to society or the advantage that the religious can extract from it, but an act: the act of believing.[8]

Many people in Latin America and in the whole world, not only people consecrated to the religious life but all people who have experienced not the sacred – which has to do with fascination and fear in the face of a force which overcomes one and serves as the foundation of established order and to which the person experiencing it belongs – but a spiritual experience (with or without calling it 'divine') which humanizes the person and leads to an encounter with the neighbour, the poor, the source of mutual humanization, 'discovers' – as Certeau says – '"something" which opens *in him* the impossibility of living without it.'[9]

The great problem or the great source of questioning and of crisis for her – and also for Liberation Christianity – will not be this calling to share the truth about Jesus and the human being in whom they believe and wager their lives, but the announcement that God fulfils the promise to free the captives and the oppressed. This promise was delayed in the fulfilling. This shows clearly in one place in Nenuca's writings. Let us seek to read it with attention:

In the streets, or under the viaducts, one lives in the dirt, exposed to the sun the rain, the cold, the wind.

Because of this, feelings of insufficiency and aloneness rise within us. It is necessary to put one's heart in God and make oneself disposed to face any season, in any sense of that word.

It is only when we go making friendships, when doubt turns into the discovery that 'something different' is taking place, that we feel better. This 'something different' the poor naturally associate with God. They come to recognize and bless God for our presence among them.

But for us, things are not tranquil. The misery is too much! It leads us each time to question the fatherhood of God. How is it possible for the Lord to be Father and allow such terrible things to happen to his children? Or does He have different categories of children, those who can live and those who can only die? Because we perceive that it won't be possible to 'free the captives'; to change the environment is going to take a long time. It won't happen before the social structures are changed. And when will that happen? At bottom, nevertheless, we feel that God wants changes. How do we

8 Michel de Certeau, *La debilidad de creer*, Buenos Aires, Katz, 2006, p. 27.
9 Certeau, *La debilidad de creer*, p. 28.

act to help in this change that God wants? While we are in search of an answer, let us rejoice with one or another who does get free. But it is so little. If it weren't for the faces, the eyes, the smiles. . . . Faces with the anxieties that we know, it is still difficult to hear God's answer to our appeals to him to save this enslaved people.

In spite of all this, the street has always been the greatest force, the way to rediscover our identity, more and more engaged in the hardness of this reality, in participating in the suffering of the poorest. Both in Recife and in São Paulo, one goes out 'with faith and courage' for our lived life.[10]

At the beginning of the passage Nenuca says: 'It is only when we go making friendships, when doubt turns into the discovery that "something different" is taking place, that we feel better. This "something different" the poor naturally associate with God. They come to recognize and bless God for our presence among them.' The first contacts between Nenuca's group and the street people are difficult and marked by suspicion on the part of the street people. But with the friendship that starts to grow, little by little, insofar as they let each other get closer physically and emotionally, this suspiciousness is transformed into the perception of the 'something different' that not only causes the street people to feel better but also causes the group of volunteers to feel better. It is necessary to give a name to this 'something different' in order to deal with it, in order to get the best possible use out of it. The poor associate it with the presence of God in their midst.

This experience of being remembered and visited by God through persons who, in the name of God, recognize in gratitude the human dignity of persons who are marginalized and excluded from human society and from the roll of persons considered 'worthy' – the story being told here in the hard experience of life under the bridges – has also taken place in many places in Latin America. This type of experience has been and continues to be the great 'spiritual force' of base communities and other kinds of community where the poor and excluded of our society meet and seek to resist the 'spirit of capitalism'.

It's just that Nenuca makes an intriguing comment immediately after saying that the poor recognized, through the presence of the volunteers, the presence of God in their midst: *But for us, things are not tranquil. The misery is too much!* That is, it is not enough to be witnesses of God's presence in the midst of the poor! Their mission is not simply to be the revelatory presence of God in the midst of the

---

10 Certeau, *La debilidad de creer*, p. 91.

poor and announce to them that God loves them or that God has compassion on them. It is more than that: it is to 'announce to them that God *fulfils his promises to free* the blind, the lame, the prisoners, the oppressed, and that they will be able to see this Salvation with their own eyes. It was this that the aged Simeon sang with Jesus in his arms!' It is a presence in their midst with a direction, a purpose: to announce a God who frees! The contradiction which disquiets them comes about between their experience and belief that God wants to free the poor from their suffering and the theology or religious discourse which permits them to explain and contextualize this experience and belief within a broader narrative. This appears more clearly in what follows in the text: 'The misery is too much! It leads us each time to *question* the fatherhood of God. How is it possible for the Lord to be Father and *allow* such terrible things to happen to his children? Or does He have different categories of children, those who can live and those who can only die?' (Italics mine.)

The conflict takes place between a traditional, premodern theology and its concrete experience on the streets and under the bridges. The theology says: God is Father and all-powerful and everything that happens in history happens in accordance with his will or permission. Nothing escapes from his knowledge and will, because he is omniscient and omnipotent. When this theology is pronounced in an abstract and generic form, there are no major problems, and the theology appears logical and coherent enough. Based on some fundamental principles and concepts – such as 'If God is God he is omniscient and omnipotent' – are deduced the secondary truths and moral and religious values which ought to guide the lives of believing persons.

Nenuca is not questioning the sexist and patriarchal aspect of the notion of the fatherhood of God – she probably had no contact with feminist theology, as she died in 1984 – but rather the contradiction between the notion that God is Father with the existence of children who 'can only die'. We all know that Christendom has produced several justifications for this contradiction, all of them from a sacrificial matrix; that is, presupposing the notion of a God who cannot save us without sacrifice, without suffering in order to pay for the sins. The sacrificial theologies transform unjust suffering into necessary payments which are exacted by God (or gods) in the form of sacrifices; they transform the victims of these injustices into sinners deserving of suffering and death. Nenuca does not accept sacrificial theology and therefore questions the theology of divine fatherhood which does not account for the concrete situation of persons or for this 'something different' which is experienced by the poor and by the volunteers.

But this questioning also reveals that she still has this premodern theology in her head. This appears when she says, 'How is it possible for the Lord to be Father and *allow* such terrible things to happen to his children?'

In the words just before these, Nenuca is describing her memory in the perspective of the third person. She is describing the memory of the experiences of the streets and under the bridges and how friendship leads the poor to recognize the presence of God in their midst and the contradiction that exists between theology and her experience. It is her memory seen by her in third-person perspective – an attitude that permits us to make, for example, a self-evaluation or a reflection about ourselves or about our thinking. But when she says, 'How is it possible, Lord . . .' she is leaving the third-person perspective and speaking in first-person perspective. It is no longer a description or a reflection but a complaint, a protest, which sprouts in the depths of her soul, in the depths of her convictions which had arisen from her religious and spiritual experience. In the name of her faith, she questions the theology with which she had been educated and had learned to interpret and express her faith.

The phrase 'How is it possible for the Lord to be Father and *allow* such terrible things to happen to his children?' shows how she still retains within herself the premodern theology which says that everything that happens is the fruit of the will or permission of God. Her problem is not with the Fatherhood of God but with the 'permission', that is, with the theology that says that history is the unfolding of the divine will, including the sufferings of the street people.

In the face of this solutionless conflict within premodern metaphysical theology, Nenuca jumps to a different theology: 'Because we perceive that it won't be possible to "free the captives"; to change the environment is going to take a long time. It won't happen before the social structures are changed. And when will that happen? At bottom, nevertheless, we feel that God wants changes. How do we act to help in this change that God wants?'

She now goes on to use a theology that satisfies her more than the first one – which she has not completely abandoned – and that is the Liberation Theology. The leverage point for this change, which permits her to make a leap without losing the foundations of her faith, is the idea or feeling that 'God wants change'. God the Father cannot be in agreement with the situation of screaming injustice, he wants change. This change in her vision of God and of history is one of the characteristics of Liberation Christianity.

In premodern worldviews and theologies, the main 'subject of history' or the only one is God. God acts or God permits! Within this worldview, there is no human 'historical subject' – a human subject who has history as its object of reflection and action – but only a divine historical subject. Insofar as history is seen as the manifestation of the divine will, hope of a qualitative and radical change in the way of life can only be realized beyond history, in 'heaven' after death. It is this which she no longer accepts, just like the modern world.

Modernity changes the place of the plenitude of the 'heaven after death' to the future which is to be constructed by the human subject through progress and/or a politico-economic revolution which would create new social structures which would be neither oppressive nor unjust. As Habermas says,

> While in the Christian West 'new times' refers to the time which is yet to come which will open up to the human being only after the Final Judgment . . . the profane conception of the modern age expresses the conviction that the future has already begun, it means the age which lives directed toward the future, which has opened up to the new things which are to come . . . the concept of progress has served not only for the secularization of eschatological hope and for the utopic opening of the horizon of expectations but equally for, with the help of the theological constructions of history, once more obstructing the future as a *source* of disquiet.[11]

Alain Touraine, for his part, says that

> modernity destroys religions, frees and usurps the image of the subject which has hitherto been prisoner to religious objectifications and to the confusion between the subject and nature, and transfers the subject from God to humans. Secularization is not the destruction of the subject but its humanization. It is not only the disenchantment of the world but the re-enchantment of the human being.[12]

These ideas show through in Nenuca's memoirs when: a) she says that the liberation of the captives will take place only with the changing

---

11 Jürgen Habermas, *O discurso filosófico da modernidade*, Lisboa, Dom Quixote, 1990, pp. 17 and 23. [English language edn: *The Philosophical Discourse of Modernity: Twelve Lectures*, trans. Frederick G. Lawrence, Cambridge, Mass., MIT Press, 1990.]

12 Alain Touraine, *Crítica da modernidade*, Petrópolis, Vozes, 1994, p. 243. [English language edn: *Critique of Modernity*, trans. David Macey, Oxford, Blackwell, 1995.]

of social structures which will still take time, that is, which will take place within historical time; and b) if it is asked 'how do we act to help in this change that God wants?', the will is God's but the action is on the part of human beings. She assumes, albeit unconsciously, one of the characteristics of Liberation Theology: a peculiar synthesis of pre-modern and modern worldviews. The basis, the project and certainty of change in history, does not come from rational argument and is not immanent in history, but is the divine will revealed in biblical tradition, a fundamental characteristic of premodern thought. But the agent of change is no longer God but the human subject; and the 'place' of the new things is not after the end of time and beyond history but the future within history.

Liberation Theology was, in a way, an attempt to negate not only the Marxist critique of religion but also the Hegelian thesis that

> only beginning with the moment when the human being ceases to project an ideal onto the Beyond is he able to realize that ideal by acting in the world, that is, to make a revolution. Conscious atheism thus necessarily leads to revolution. Ergo, theism and revolution are mutually exclusive, and any attempt whatsoever at synthesis can only lead to a misunderstanding which will be revealed when the time comes for genuine action.[13]

It is necessary also to point out a characteristic of Liberation Christianity with regard to the historic subject of liberation. Whereas in liberalism the principal agent is the bourgeois and in Marxism it is the proletariat or the revolutionary party, in Liberation Christianity the poor are the subject of their own liberation. This appears for example in the themes of the interchurch meetings of the ecclesial base communities of Brazil. At the first of these meetings, held in Vitória in 1975, the theme was 'CEBs: A Church which is Born of the People by the Holy Spirit'. The second meeting, held in 1976, had as its theme 'CEBs: Church, People who Journey' and dealt with the engagement of the CEBs in social struggles. At the third meeting in 1979, the theme had evolved to 'CEBs: People which Liberates Itself'; and at the fourth meeting, the last one held before Nenuca's death, the theme was 'CEBs: The People United, Seed of a New Society'. These themes reflect the optimism that was in the air at the time, regarding the possibility or near-certainty of the liberation of the poor. The big question was when

---

13 Alexandre Kojève, *Introdução à leitura de Hegel*, Rio de Janeiro, Contraponto-EdUERJ, 2002, p. 204.

and not whether it was possible or not. In what Nenuca wrote, this appears in the question, 'And when will this take place?'

No one thought of questioning or doubting the possibility that the liberation of the poor will be possible within history, for this would be to negate the power of God to carry out, through his 'chosen' people – the poor and the CEBs – his will to liberate and to create a new heaven and a new earth.

The problem is that history doesn't happen according to religious promises or certain interpretations of religious texts, nor in accordance with our best desires. Crisis always comes to persons who, in spite of trusting theologies and meta-narratives of liberation, have eyes and ears open to the everyday lives of persons who suffer. Nenuca, who was more open to the reality of persons than to theories or books, speaks of the crisis that emerges even in this new theology. She says,

> While we are seeking the answer [to the question of how to act to bring about change] we rejoice with one or another who gets free. *But it is so little.* If it were not for the faces, the eyes, the smiles . . . In the face of the anxieties which we know, it is still difficult to hear God's answer to our appeals for the salvation of this enslaved people.

The words 'But it is so little' are of profound existential intensity. This is no mere conclusion at the end of logical argument or of a well-executed analysis. It is this, but not only this! This lament is the expression of a synthesis of reason and emotion: the rational statement that those who get free are few in number and the expression of sorrow and frustration that comes from the bottom of her heart, for they are 'so few!'

What brought about her crisis is not some contradiction internal in theological discourse or the discovery of a defective articulation between the propositions of Liberation Theology and the Christian-biblical tradition. The crisis in reflection and the pain come from the statement that 'in the face of the anxieties that we know, it is still difficult to hear God's answer to our appeals. . . .' The theoretical answers about the possibilities of the future which should be guaranteed by the promises of God revealed in the Bible are not enough for her in the face of so much suffering by so many people for so much time. More than that, it seems that she is beginning to doubt the optimistic affirmations of Liberation Theology.

Different answers to the crisis of utopia

The crisis that results from Liberation Theology's being out of step with experience, which Nenuca told of in the early 1980s, became clearer for many others with the fall of the Berlin Wall and the defeat of the socialist bloc. The reason for this is that significant sectors of Liberation Christianity had seen in socialism the way to overcoming the injustices of capitalism.

Clodovis Boff, for example, wrote a few months prior to the fall of the Berlin Wall that

> socialism is not a mere project or simple historic ideal but is the *expression of the real process of history* . . . There is objectively, then, no other way out. For the rest, the people is being pushed in this direction by reality itself, as is shown by the historic process of the nations which have emancipated themselves most recently.

And he concludes his reflections by affirming that 'the ideal of the "communion of goods", of which socialism is the modern form, was and continues to be the great social ideal of Christians' and that 'it is clear that Christianity is re-encountering its socialist roots. In the meantime, socialism is opening up to the ethico-religious dimension.'[14]

I do not wish to discuss here whether there is or is not an affinity between socialism and Christianity or whether there is a real process of history pushing us in a given direction but only to show that the impact of the defeat of the socialist bloc is clearly present in the themes of the interchurch meetings of the CEBs. In 1986, the sixth interchurch had as its theme 'CEBs: People of God in Search of the Promised Land', and the seventh meeting (which brought together more than 2,500 persons from 19 Latin American countries and 12 churches, in July of 1989 and before the fall of the Wall), had as its theme 'CEBs: People of God in Latin America on the Way to Liberation'. These themes still express continuity in the 'optimistic' line in relation to the liberation of the poor. At the eighth meeting in 1992 the theme was 'CEBs: Oppressed Cultures and Evangelization in Latin America'. At the ninth meeting in 1997 it was 'CEBs: Life and Hope among the Masses'. At the tenth, it was 'CEBs, People of God: 2000 Years on the Journey'. This reveals a significant modification of perspective, a modification which reveals frustration with the unfulfilled messianic expectation or with the unrealized historic expectation.

---

14 Clodovis Boff, *Cartas teológicas sobre o socialismo*, Petrópolis, Vozes, 1989, pp. 130 and 139–40.

In the face of the 'crisis of paradigms' caused by the distance between the expectations generated by the 'messianic' narratives and the reality experienced in concrete life, the intellectuals and the leaders of social movements and CEBs were and still are called upon to give an answer. The way this crisis is resolved will mark or significantly influence the future of Liberation Christianity in Latin America. I wish to mention briefly some of the proposals that we find today.

One solution is to propose a new theme (such as, for example, the discussion of new historical or theological subjects – indigenous peoples, blacks, women, etc. – or intercultural dialogue) as a new theological and ecclesial challenge, without responding adequately to the fundamental crisis of a messianic expectation unfulfilled or discussing how liberation is understood today. This can be understood as a way of changing the focus with the introduction of new themes which, by being new, end up calling attention to themselves. With this I do not wish to say that new themes and challenges are not important, but only to point to the fact that these new approaches and new themes often aid in the non-facing of one of the fundamental problems of Liberation Christianity which is that of the frustration of messianic expectation – something similar to what happened to the 'Emmaus disciples'.

A second type of solution is that of explicitly maintaining the hope of Liberation Christianity by reaffirming certain 'metaphysical truths' and from them reconstructing, with or without new theoretical or scientific arguments, the validity of the messianic expectation. I wish to present here what appear to me to be two theoretical options within that same line.

Benedito Ferraro, a long-time consultant for the interchurch meetings, wrote regarding the Ninth Meeting, of 1997:

> What could be seen and sensed at the Ninth Interchurch was the reaffirmation of the utopia of having space and a place for everyone . . . Here is found one of the great challenges raised by the meeting of the CEBs: how to re-activate the dream, the utopia of a society which accepts everyone independently of colour, sex, culture, or religion . . . This search for a society where all would fit in continues to be the great utopia . . . It is on the basis of the struggles of the popular movements, the struggles of women, blacks, Indians, children that the new dream, which is always also an old dream, keeps arising on the horizon: the creation of an 'Earthly Paradise', of the 'Land Without Afflictions',[15] of the 'Classless Society'.[16]

---

15 Or 'Land Without Evils' (*Terra sem Males*) (translator's note).
16 Benedito Ferraro, 'IX Encontro Intereclesial de CEBs: festa da inclusão

He does not question the notion of utopia, nor does he question the historical possibility, defended by modern reason, of building within history the 'earthly paradise' (of the biblical tradition), the 'land without evil' (of Guarani tradition), of the 'classless society' (from Marxism). Its objective is to reaffirm the validity of this utopia and reactivate this dream and the struggles for its construction. The God who reveals Godself in the Bible, in the original religions of Latin America, and in the social movements committed to the life of the poor and to justice, is presented as the ultimate foundation of the validity of this utopia and of this meta-narrative.

Leonardo Boff, for his part, seeks to reaffirm 'utopia' in the name of new scientific theories and in dialogue with them. Building on the cosmological thesis that there must exist some infinitesimal fine-tuning of the parameters for the stars to have formed and for life to have originated, he declares that

> the understanding of it presupposes that the universe is not blind but rather filled with purpose and intention. Even a well-known atheist astrophysicist such as Fred Hoyle acknowledges that evolution can only be understood on the premises that there must exist a supremely intelligent Agent. God, the name for this Agent, a supremely intelligent master ruler, is umbilically involved in the evolutionary and cosmogenic processes.[17]

Contrary to thoughts which draw on historic facts in order to affirm that history does not have a pre-determined sense or that history will not lead to harmony and plenitude (the Kingdom of God or the 'Land Without Afflictions'), L. Boff seeks a broader vision of history – the whole evolutionary and cosmogenic process – in order to affirm that there is a supreme intelligent and ordering Agent behind everything that happens in the universe.

He makes a leap from this premise to theological argumentation:

> It is here that the Christian faith comes in, as the spearhead of cosmic consciousness. Faith sees at the omega point of evolution the Christ of faith, he who is believed in and announced as the head of the cosmos and of the Church, the meeting point of all beings. If

---

e recriação da utopia. Um olhar de esperança', *Revista Eclesiástica Brasileira*, Petrópolis, 57/228 (1997), pp. 811–16, p. 814 is cited.

17 L. Boff, *Ecologia: grito da Terra, grito dos pobres*, São Paulo, Ática, 1995, p. 226. [English language edn: *Cry of the Earth, Cry of the Poor*, Maryknoll, NY, Orbis Books, 1997.]

what faith proclaims is neither mere ideology nor pure unconscious fantasy, then this must show itself somehow in the evolutionary process of the universe.[18]

With this he is able to conclude his argumentation by saying, 'Eco-spiritually, hope gives us assurance that, in spite of all the threats of destruction which the aggression machine of the human species has set up and used against Gaia, *the good and beneficent future* is guaranteed because this Cosmos and this Earth are of the Spirit and the Word'.[19]

These two proposals share a common presupposition with each other and with premodern theology: the metaphysical conception of truth and a meta-narrative of history. That is, the presupposition of an order in history or the cosmos which is already written and inscribed in the evolutional and historical process and which can be known objectively through the natural sciences, the science or philosophy of history, or by revelation. This knowledge shows us that utopia, the Kingdom of God, or the Land without Afflictions will be established definitively and surely within history.

One of the problems with this apparent solution is that the concrete sufferings and anxieties of persons remain unanswered or undervalued owing to their smallness in the face of the evolution of the cosmos and the long history of the building of utopia. Or they are simply seen as the 'labour pains' of the new world, that is, pain which is necessary. Furthermore, with this 'optimism' it obstructs, as Habermas says, 'the future as a *source* of disquiet'.[20] That is, we don't need to worry about the future because it is already guaranteed.

Another problem with this type of metaphysical thinking is that it can lead to a kind of left-wing sacrificialism, requiring sacrifices in the name of the struggle for a society without sacrifice.[21] We can find an example of this in the remarks of José M. Vigil at the 'Forum on the Theology of the Liberation of the Children of Abraham', which took place in Bari, Italy (7–9 December 2005), which brought together representatives of Judaism, Christianity, and Islam. After saying that the absolute supremacy of utopia is the second essential dimension of the liberating vision, the author affirms that there is a liberating perspective when the utopia of liberation is on the horizon of the

---

18 Boff, *Ecologia*, p. 273.
19 Boff, *Ecologia*, p. 306, italics mine.
20 Habermas, *O discurso filosófico da modernidade*, p. 23.
21 See for example Franz Hinkelammert, *Crítica de la razón utópica*, Bilbao, Desclée de Brouwer, 2002; *Sacrifícios humanos e sociedade ocidental: Lúcifer e a Besta*, São Paulo, Paulus, 1995.

journey, a messianic hope and promise which attracts those who are on the journey and gives them the power to overcome the obstacles and temptations which pull them out of the journey. If the utopia is absolute, everything can and should be sacrificed for it. With this in mind, Vigil says:

> Abraham entered obediently into the journey with no fixed goal, knowing only that he should journey toward the 'land which I will show you'. This Promised Land, which lies ahead but not exactly within hand's reach, if not a horizon from which there is strength for the journey, is also the 'absolute' Utopia by means of which those on the journey are able to leave behind and postpone (sacrifice) everything, even one's own son Isaac. To make possible the realization of the Promise, to live and struggle for the promised New Land . . . constitutes the task of human life in its mission on earth.[22]

Being disposed to sacrifice everything including one's own son for a society without sacrifice (utopia) is a consequence of the illusion and the pretension of building a full and absolute society with human actions.

These two types of solution to the crisis – that of changing the focus and that of reaffirming the expectation of realizing utopia – are attempts to maintain the validity and vitality of Liberation Christianity by maintaining the messianic expectation of full liberation of the poor and oppressed within history. We can say that this line is the best known and most accepted one among the communities and activists of Liberation Christianity, since it reaffirms both the power of God as liberator and the guarantee that the deepest desires of persons of good will be met.

Nevertheless, this line of thinking is not the only one present within Liberation Christianity in Latin America. A third type of solution has been presented by what I call the 'DEI[23] School' (Franz Hinkelammert, Hugo Assmann, Julio de Santa Ana, and others), which criticizes the transcendental illusion of modernity,[24] the pretension of modern reason and Western civilization to construct a perfect society within history. This is the pretension which, as we have seen, always leads to sacrificial demands.[25]

---

22 José Maria Vigil, 'El camino de liberación de las fes del Mediterráneo', *Alternativas: revista de análisis y reflexión teológica*, Manágua, 13/31 (2006), pp. 165–78; the quotation is from p. 170.

23 DEI is the acronym of the name of a study centre in Costa Rica, Departamente Ecuménico de Investigaciones.

24 The principal work along these lines is Hinkelammert, *Crítica*.

25 See for example, Assmann and Hinkelammert, *Idolatria do mercado*,

These authors defend the thesis that utopia is a condition for us to be able to elaborate theories of action, an epistemological necessity for everyone who would intervene in society or in nature. Even neoliberals who criticize the very idea of utopia need to create the transcendental or utopic concept of 'perfectly competitive market' or 'totally free market' in order to be able to elaborate hypotheses which orient their interventions in the economic and political areas. Utopia (perfect society, perfect market, perfect body, etc.) allows us to see what is deficient in that which presently exists and allows us to sketch strategies of intervention in order to get closer to the model of perfection. For example, an engineer who wishes to make a more efficient motor needs to have in mind a motor that uses no energy at all and then get as close as possible to this ideal model.

In the case of engineering, he knows that his ultimate objective is impossible because it goes against the laws of thermodynamics, but he has no existential problem about it. But social agents and movements, whether pro-capitalist or anti-capitalist, easily forget the historic non-attainability of utopia – and the secret of the attraction of the great utopias is exactly in this forgetting. For it is this forgetting that fires up hope for the full realization of our desires. Freud said that the power of religion resides in desire, and here we can paraphrase him and say: the power of utopia is in the desire.

In this same line of criticism of the illusion of modernity, we find a fourth type of answer to the crisis, which puts the focus more on everyday life, in microsocial and interpersonal relations. Ivone Gebara, taking into consideration her everyday experience – she works and lives in a very poor neighbourhood – wrote in 1990:

I ask myself whether our 'discourse' to the poor about their liberation, about the conquest of land, about justice . . . might not be getting flawed by a fine idealism or by hope without adequate analysis of the objective conditions of our history? . . . I dare to think that we ought to start the process of refusing 'cheap comfort', as did Rachel (Jer. 31.15) in refusing comfort in the face of the death of her children. She preferred to continue in lamentation and weeping, in other words, in the reality of her pain, rather than

---

Petrópolis, Vozes, 1989; Assmann, *Crítica à lógica da exclusão*, São Paulo, Paulus, 1994; Hinkelammert, *Sacrifícios humanos y la sociedad occidental: Lúcifer y la Bestia*, San José (Costa Rica), Dei, 1991; Jung Mo Sung, *Teologia e economia: repensando a TL e as utopias*, Petrópolis, Vozes, 1994; and *Sujeito e sociedades complexas: para repensar os horizontes utópicos*, Petrópolis, Vozes, 2002.

'swallow down' an anaesthetic that might create illusions and false hopes.[26]

In writing this, Gebara publicly criticized the majority within Liberation Theology and, little by little, went on to elaborate another type of theology in order to understand and express her faith and her option for the poor and for oppressed persons and groups. This courageous article must have cost her uncomprehending rejection. After all, for the optimists realism appears to be pessimism. For that reason, in an article published in 1991, Gebara says:

> I do not feel myself to be a pessimist, but I am more and more disturbed by the unrealistic discourse of the theologians and of some social scientists who think to modify reality through their writings. The theologians . . . speak of their desires as though they were realities and create anxieties in the less critical readers, who become frustrated insofar as they do not find in their lives what the theologians are talking about. Theology is speaking of the 'not yet' based on the 'already', that is, based on the real life of the different groups.[27]

The thinkers of the 'DEI school' and also Ivone Gebara have criticized the transcendental illusion of neoliberal capitalism and its sacrificial demands in the name of the absolutizing of the market, of the 'idolatry of the market'. This criticism of the transcendental illusion also applies to some sectors of Liberation Christianity which believe they can construct within history a society that will be fully harmonious, with full justice and solidarity; but this does not amount to a criticism of Liberation Christianity as such, much less a call to abandon the struggle for a society with more justice and solidarity or for a bodily life with more dignity for all persons. It only means accepting the limits of history and of the human condition and undertaking a struggle for other forms of interpersonal and social life and other ways of organizing society which will be more just and humane, with more solidarity. For this group, the value and validity of Liberation Christianity are not based on its promise to build utopia but on the justice of the struggle itself.

---

26 Ivone, Gebara, 'Hora de ficar: dificuldades das religiosas na evangelização em meio a um povo empobrecido', *Vida Pastoral*, São Paulo, 160 (1991), p. 4.

27 Ivone, Gebara, 'Espiritualidade: escola ou busca cotidiana?' *Vida Pastoral*, São Paulo, 164 (1992), p. 9; see also, by the same author, *Rompendo o silêncio. Uma fenomenologia feminista do mal*, Petrópolis, Vozes, 2000.

Coming out of this reflection, we can ask ourselves: is it possible to maintain the validity and vitality of Liberation Christianity while accepting the limits of the human condition and the insuperable contradictions of history? Or is Liberation Christianity so connected with the promise of liberation that it cannot survive without 'forgetting' that utopia will be fully realized within history?

'The faces, the eyes, the smiles . . . '

And how does Nenuca solve her crisis? We need to remember that the crisis we are talking about is not a crisis of the meaning of her life but the crisis that arises from the conflict between her life of faith and the religious discourse she has available for explaining this life.

I do not believe that she solved the crisis, for she did not find another theological discourse to replace the premodern theology and the Liberation Theology with which she was telling and explaining her experiences and her difficulties. She would not let herself be convinced by the theology of 'God the Father who allows these things to happen' and neither does she nourish the illusion that, with liberation, the future will be wonderful. Still less does she let herself be taken by pessimism, nihilism, or indifference as defence mechanisms in the face of pain and anxiety, nor does she allow herself to be attracted by 'new loves', new themes or projects which would lead her astray from the faces and the eyes of the street people.

Theology is not the source of her motivation or of her identity. Theology, like other philosophical or social theories, can speak about or in favour of the struggle for the poor and by the poor, but it is always the discourse of an outside observer, in a third-person perspective. A different theology might facilitate her understanding of her experience and her anxiety, but the lack of one does not immobilize her, nor does it take her faith away.

She stays realistic at the same time that she seeks to find power with which to stay on in the struggle. She says, 'In spite of all this – that is, recognizing all the difficulties, frustrations and anxieties – the street has always been the greatest force.' And what is it about the street that gives her the power to keep going? We can find the answer in the words that she lets out between two negative statements: 'But it is so little. If it were not for the faces, the eyes, the smiles . . . In the face of the anxieties which we know, it is still difficult to hear God's answer to our appeals for the salvation of this enslaved people.' Between the statements that it is so little and that it is difficult to hear God's answer, she lets out the words 'if it were not for the faces, the eyes, the smiles . . . ' of poor persons, prostitutes, the young and so many other persons who are to be found in the gutters, under the bridges, or in other places where the poorest people find a nook or cranny in which to survive. It is the 'something different' which arises from the friendship with these persons whom, however damaged they are, she recognizes as human, that makes her keep going.

The choice to keep working, 'in spite of all this' is not the fruit of an irrational or meaningless choice, much less the result of a sacrificial choice. She does not sacrifice her life for a utopia which she believes will be realized in the future, not does she assume the posture of self-sacrifice as living a life of pain and sorrow only in order to identify with the Jesus who suffers on the cross. It is something positive that maintains her in her choice: the humanizing experience that arises from an encounter with the poorest people and friendship with them. This is the experience which permits people to meet one another as subjects meeting subjects and not subjects meeting others who have been reduced to the condition of objects of observation, manipulation, or conquest.[28]

This 'something different' – the faces, the eyes, the smiles – is not a mere consolation, a crumb which one gets hold of following the sensation of failure. It is the foundation, the base, the 'bedrock' on which she reconstructs the meaning of her life and her struggle; it is the 'firm place' from which she takes her leap of faith which will orient her everyday life and actions. For this reason she says that it is in the encounter with these persons that they, the community, re-encounter their identity: 'In spite of all this, the street has always been the greatest force, the way for us to re-encounter our identity, more and more engaged in the hardness of this reality, in our participation in the suffering of the poorest. Both in Recife and in São Paulo, we went out "with faith and courage" for our experiences.'

When she talks about how to re-encounter her identity she is speaking from a first-person perspective. She is not using an observer's perspective, which is a third-person perspective, in order to see the reach, the limits, and the contradictions of the option for the poor, whether in line with premodern theology or in the perspective of Liberation Theology.

When she speaks of the small result or of the difficulty of hearing an answer from God she is using the perspective of an observer. But when

---

28 On this question see Sung, *Sujeito*, ch. 3 (The subject as transcendentality within real life).

she says 'if it were not for the faces, the eyes, the smiles . . .' or when she says 'we went out "with faith and courage" for our experiences', she is using a first-person perspective. And in the first person I do not ask about the reach of a particular action or about what kind of action will lead to fulfilling my intention, but I ask about what kind of action I *ought* to carry out in order to be in accordance with my intentions and with my identity. And as we have seen above, for Nenuca, '*We who feel called to follow him have nothing else to do*. Like Him, we have to go to human beings, those most deeply immersed in the darkness of death, to announce to them the Sun of Life.'

Spiritual experience does not call for coherence in relation to a particular theory or theology but coherence in relation to the foundational experience, 'the first love', the fundamental choice which has marked and modified one's life.

This oscillation between the third and first persons, which are never confused with one another and never appear at the same time, is owing to the fact that, as Akeel Bilgrame says, 'we cannot be at the same time *agents* and *observers* or predictors of what we ourselves and our own minds are going to do to us or what they will "lead us" to do. As long as we are agents we ask what it *would be necessary* to do, and we say what we *commit ourselves* to do by way of our intentions.'[29]

Someone might remind us: 'But the promised liberation is delayed!' This statement, however, is that of an observer who measures the distance between the hypothesis of liberation and the reality of the concrete life of the poor. And Liberation Christianity, like other religious and spiritual movements in history, does not find its power and its greatest significance in the statements of observers, in discourse from a third-person perspective, but in the commitment of agents who have experienced an event which permits them a new perception of reality and a new relation with the world and which leads them to take on commitments and carry out particular actions.[30]

There are many persons and groups which, like Nenuca's group, continue to live their commitment to oppressed persons and groups in spite of the frustrations with their expectations and the insufficiency of theologies to explain their faith and praxis in today's world, in spite

---

29 Akeel Bilgrami, 'Interpretando una distinción', in Homi Bhabha and W. J. T. Mitchell (ed.), *Edward Said: continuando la conversación*, Buenos Aires, Barcelona, México, Paidós, 2006, pp. 45–58; the quotation is from p. 55. [English language edn: *Edward Said: Continuing the Conversation*, Chicago, University of Chicago Press, 2004.]

30 See the concept of 'permission' in Certeau, *La debilidad de creer*, pp. 215–17.

of the official doctrines of their churches and in spite of theologies which insist on the absolute truth of their (conservative or progressive) dogmas which are petrified by time. These persons live their faith because they continue to feel called and are unable not to follow it. This is the power of Liberation Christianity. Theologies, historical analyses, sociologies, and other reflections understand this movement better and contribute to this journey only insofar as they take seriously words like Nenuca's, which show that theoretical or linguistic theories cannot account for this spirit which moves these people. That is, insofar as they do not reduce this experience to a set of principles and categories which are assumed a priori and do not have the pretension to exhaust or reduce this experience to some kind of rational explanation of a sociological, psychological, historical, or theological kind or even a store of knowledge that is used in an interdisciplinary way.

Freedom and mystery

Someone could still ask: But God's promises of liberation will be fulfilled? That is, are God's promises true? After all, many entered into this struggle or stayed in it because of these promises. This kind of question presupposes a notion of truth with which we read scientific or religious texts. People like Nenuca do not wait for a satisfactory answer to this question in order to remain firm, with 'faith and courage'. But it is also necessary to give answers. I think that one cannot give a quick answer in yes or no terms, nor yet in terms of a little bit now and in fullness in the 'parousia'. It is necessary to get deeper and question the question of truth itself which underlies the question. As this question – fundamental for theologians, philosophers, historians, and other scholars of religion – calls for many more pages, I wish simply to introduce here a provocative text by Vattimo:

> The truth which, according to Jesus, will make us free is not the objective truth of the sciences, much less the truth of theology: the Bible is not a book of cosmology, much less a manual of anthropology or theology. The revelation of Scripture does not reside in making us know what we are, what God is made of, what is the nature of things or what are the laws of geometry and things like that, as though we could save ourselves through 'knowledge' of the truth. The only truth of Scripture reveals itself as that which in the course of time cannot be the object of demystification – since it is not

an experimental statement, or a logical one, or a metaphysical one, but a practical calling – it is the truth of love, of *caritas*.[31]

If the promise of liberation has something to do with the truth which will make us free, and if this truth has something to do with love rather than analysis or historical prediction, what is the guarantee of liberation? The almost permanent recurrence of utopian horizons, such as the 'earthly paradise', the 'land without afflictions', or the 'classless society' or the new cosmological or scientific theories are not a secure platform for affirming that history tends toward or is 'designed' in connection with a 'happy ending'. Much less do these things guarantee the possibility of constructing within history the desired plenitude of life.

Western tradition has always based its thought on the notion of order and sought the foundation of this order. God has always been sought or speculated about precisely as the foundation of this order – seen as static in the premodern world and evolutionary in the modern world. For this reason, in the above-cited cosmological argumentation of Leonardo Boff we find the reference to God as 'the name for this supremely intelligent and *ordering* Agent' (italics mine). But this is not the only way to understand human reality. Comblin affirms that in the biblical tradition God is not understood as the foundation of order but as love. And 'love does not found order but disorder. Love breaks every structure of order. Love founds freedom and, in consequence, disorder. Sin is a consequence of the love of God.'[32] And when the Bible says that God is love, it is affirming that the human calling is freedom, that this is more than a quality or an attribute of the human being but is humanity's very reason for being. 'That God is love and that the human calling is freedom are the two sides of the same reality, the two aspects of the same movement.'[33]

If it is not possible for us to live in freedom without the possibility of evil (ethically speaking), we can say in a religious way of speaking that God made the world in such a way that sin is an inevitable possibility. For this reason, Comblin comes back to a text in the Apocalypse, 'I stand at the door and knock. If someone hears my voice and opens the door, I will come in to him and dine with him, and he with me' (Rev. 3.20); and Comblin says, 'If nobody opens, God accepts defeat know-

---

31 Richard Rorty and Gianni Vattimo, *El futuro de la religión: solidaridad, caridad, ironía*, ed. Santiago Zabala, Buenos Aires, Paidós, 2006, p. 75.

32 José Comblin, *Cristãos rumo ao século XXI: nova caminhada de libertação*, São Paulo, Paulus, 1996, p. 65.

33 Comblin, *Cristãos*, p. 67.

ing that his creation has failed. God created a world that could fail.'[34]
In other words, there is nothing that guarantees that human history
will end well, that good will definitively defeat evil within history; not
even the notion of God or the incarnation of God is such a guarantee.

This kind of theology seems a good bit more compatible with spiritual experience and the social commitment of so many persons and
groups who continue in the struggle, 'in spite of all this'. For the original
source of Liberation Christianity is the spiritual experience that allows
one to see an image of God that is not based on sacrificial demands or
on indifference to the suffering of persons, an image of the good God
'who does not want this' and who calls us to take sides in the face of
unjust reality and to change human relations and social structures.
The utopic horizon of a society without oppression and injustice arises
from this experience and proceeds from it. And the desire that this
horizon be realized historically leads or could lead to the illusion of a
theology or a science that claims to guarantee the realization of this
utopia within history.

Theories – whether theological, cosmological, or social – that claim
to uncover the order that moves reality and to predict the meaning
and goal of human history and of nature end up falling into the kind
of metaphysical thinking which, in order to get closure as a system of
thought, needs to negate the reality and drama of human suffering,
especially the suffering of innocents. Against this temptation, I think
it is important, as Gebara says, to refuse 'cheap comfort' as Rachel did
(Jer. 31.15) and remain – at least for a significant time – in weeping and
lamentation, in the reality of suffering. False hopes can immobilize
– for the future is seen as already guaranteed, and no longer serves as a
source of disquiet (Habermas) – and also can lead to sacrificial theologies which present a God who demands sacrifices.

The only way for us to avoid the temptation of modernity to reduce
all the mysteries of life to a scientific or theoretical problem to be
solved is to remain in anguish before the suffering of the innocent and
the insoluble crisis provoked by the reality of evil and the confession
of faith in a God who is love and freedom. Life has mysteries – like
the mystery of evil – which are not reducible to theoretical explana-
tions. The fundamental mysteries of human life continue and will continue to be mysteries in spite of all intellectual attempts. It is for this
reason that the truth which can set us free is not a truth that explains
and solves the 'puzzles' of reality, but an ethical appeal to love and
solidarity.

---

34 Comblin, *Cristãos*, p. 66.

Theoretical systems, even those that admit to being postmodern, tend to close in on themselves as systems which aim to account for a reality or for an object of study. One of the ways of avoiding this tendency and temptation is always to be open to the appeal of the 'other' who suffers, who does not see their pain contemplated by a theoretical system or does not find in that system any solidarity with their pain. And this is especially valid for theology and for other studies that have as their object of reflection the religiosity of the people.

After these reflections, we come back to the question in the title: Has Liberation Christianity failed? I think a certain kind of Liberation Christianity, the kind that made the promise of building utopia its principal force and motivation, is in a deep crisis, not to say that it has failed. But the spiritual force and identity of significant sectors of Liberation Christianity have not been based on this transcendental illusion. For many, even if they reproduced the optimistic theological discourse which was dominant, the spiritual power of its Christianity came and comes from the experience which allows them to see and relate to the world, society, and persons in a new way. It is this spirituality that leads them to seek coherence with their identity in personal and social commitment to the persons who suffer the most.

For people like Nenuca and her companions, who in spite of everything continue in the struggle 'with faith and courage', the question about the failure of the utopia of Liberation Christianity is not the most fundamental question, for it is a question in third-person perspective, that of an external observer. The most fundamental question is how we can be coherent with our 'first love', how to live in accordance with the experience which has given human meaning to our lives for which reason we feel called to walk on this journey.

This journey, with its difficulties and its joys, calls for a religious discourse able to account for this experience, even while knowing that it will always be provisory and insufficient. For those who feel part of this Liberation Christianity, even if they are not church members, the challenge is – as Gutiérrez says – 'to find a language about God in the midst of the hunger for bread of millions of human beings, in the midst of the humiliation of the races considered inferior, of discrimination against women.'[35]

But we must not forget that, even when we get to this discourse, it will only be a discourse, and that spiritual power does not reside in the

---

35 Gustavo Gutiérrez, *Falar de Deus a partir do sofrimento do inocente: uma reflexão sobre o livro de Jó*, Petrópolis, Vozes, 1987, p. 164. [English language edn: *On Job: God-Talk and the Suffering of the Innocent*, Maryknoll, NY, Orbis Books, 1987.]

discourse but in the experience which continually protests and talks back to the images of God and of the human being that are presented by the theories. For the pain of injustice and of hunger and the joy of the encounter among persons who mutually recognize each other in grace transcend any human language. They are above and beyond any and every symbol.

Index of Names and Subjects

Albert, Michel 67, 93
Alves, Rubem 1
Anderson, Perry 83
Aquinas, St Thomas 8
Aristotle 67
Arrow, Kenneth 93
Assisi, St Francis 49
Assmann, Hugo 12, 49, 51, 62, 71, 73, 94, 109–16, 144

Becker, Gary 81
Bilgrami, Akeel 149
Boff, Clodovís 140
Boff, Leonardo 49, 70
Bresser Pereira, Luiz 88–9
Buarque, Cristovam 11, 31, 52, 79
Buchanan, James 81

Camdessus, Michel 20–1, 94n
Campos, Roberto 17, 70
capitalism 2, 3, 12, 14, 48, 56, 66, 68, 82–9, 93, 94, 97, 109, 120, 140, 146
 critique 22, 111, 115
Capra, Fritjof 114, 116–20
Certeau, Michel de 132–4
Comblin, José 26, 54–5, 127–8, 151–2
commodity(ies) 1–3, 7, 18, 50, 93
 fetish(ism) 2, 47
competition 14, 21–2, 37–9, 42,

57, 58, 59, 60, 61, 62, 67, 69, 74, 81, 85, 87, 95, 107
consumption 10, 35, 36, 38, 65, 77, 78, 87–9, 91–2, 102, 104, 125–6
 level 42
 limitless 29, 72, 92
 mimetic character 48
 pattern(s) 34, 79

death(s) 9–10, 12–3, 16, 17, 18, 26, 45, 56, 132, 135, 137
 life after 14, 24
demand(s) 12, 27, 30, 31n, 34, 79, 98, 112, 144, 146
 sacrificial 64, 152
dependency theory 110, 112
desire(s) 1–4, 14, 32–3, 67, 74–5, 92, 106, 119, 120, 145
 consumption 38, 65
 encouraged 46
 object(s) 1, 36, 46, 59
 satisfaction of all 57, 59
 satisfaction of basic 48
development 35, 39–42, 65, 79, 84, 88–9
 economic 33–4, 48, 104
 myth 34, 52
 social 70
 technical 57
dignity 6, 10, 54, 57, 61, 75, 101, 102, 146

fundamental 25–6
human 24, 27, 45–7, 50, 97, 134
Drucker, Peter 16, 66, 125
Durkheim 72

economic(s) 1, 4, 63, 85, *see also* globalization, economic; globalization, economy
  adjustment(s) 17, 21, 34, 67, 80
  growth 7, 13, 31, 40, 42, 66, 70, 77, 81, 86, 88–9
  policy(ies) 15, 48
  production 37, 59, 79
  religion 12, 63, 111, 112
  theology 2, 8–12, 22, 76, *see also* theology
  theory(ies) 32, 80–1, 86, 90, 111
efficiency 3, 21, 61, 70–1, 85, 92–4, 95, 102–3, 105, 107–8, 125, 126
Europe 78, 79, 90
evil(s) 12, 16, 72, 75, 142, 151–2
  economic and social 70, 72
  fundamental 15
  transfiguration 91
exclusion 18, 27, 65–6, 73, 75, 86
  process 66
  social 3–4, 35, 51–3, 68, 81, 87, 89, 91, 98

Ferraro, Benedito 141
First World 42, 74–5, 101
Freud, Sigmund 145
Friedman, Milton 15
Fromm, Eric 22, 49, 72
Fukuyama, Francis 13–4, 18, 36, 56–60, 92–3
Furtado, Celso 11, 34–5, 39
Fuser, Cláudia 30

G-22 (G-20 Plus) 103, 105, 106, 109, 126
Galbraith, John Kenneth 11, 43, 52n, 69, 87
Gebara, Ivone 145–6, 152
Gilder, George 56, 91–2
Girard, René 35, 40, 44, 45, 49, 57, 59, 62–3
globalization 7, 11, 19–22, 76, 122, *see also* economic(s)
  economic 115, 117–8, 120, 121, 126
  economy 14–5, 17, 51, 66, 77
God 23–4, 26–8, 71–3, 75, 91, 95–8, 98, 122–3, 133–9, 150–2
  existence 8
  image(s) 8–9, 25, 64, 115, 154
González, Antonio 122–5
government 73, 81, 87, 88, 90, 105–9, 119
  role 17
Guanaes, Nizan 46
Gutiérrez, Gustavo 100, 101, 108, 131n, 153

Habermas, Jürgen 13n, 137, 143, 152
Hayek, Friedrich 15, 36–9, 46–7, 59–61, 70
Hegel 57
Heller, Agnes 109
Hinkelammert, Franz 8n, 32, 39, 44n, 62, 110, 112, 115n, 144
historical project(s) 112, 115, 121
hope(s) 8, 29, 49, 64, 105, 137, 141, 144, 145, 152
  eschatological 12, 36, 56
  utopian 13, 18
Horkheimer, Max 22, 72, 96

idolatry 1, 4, 21–2, 72, 75,
90–1, 96–8, 105
critique 23–5, 27
market 63, 71, 95, 109–14,
126, 146, see also market
individual(s) 41, 60, 80–2, 87–8,
97, 109
liberalism 84
rational 92
inequality(ies) 68, 122
social 35, 52, 69, 71, 77, 87,
123–4, 126
injustice(s) 6, 31, 54, 64, 73,
121–3, 135, 136, 140, 152,
154, see also justice
International Monetary Fund
(IMF) 17, 21, 42, 80, 90, 119

Jesus 8, 9, 20, 26–7, 28–9, 33,
69, 72, 74, 75, 133, 148
Christ 25
death 90
meeting 130–1
Messiah 25–6
poor 105
resurrection 23–5, 49, 95
sacrifice 45
Josephus, Flavius 23
justice 23–4, 26, 40, 71, 142,
146, see also injustice(s)
proof 26
social 45
transcendental 69

kingdom 21
freedom 26, 41, 80
God 19–22, 25–8, 80, 96, 99,
121–2, 124, 127, 142, 143, see
also reign of God
Koetler, Philip 32, 41
Krugman, Paul 117

Latouche, Serge 13
Libânio, João 107–8, 124
liberation Christianity 4, 129–
30, 133, 136, 138, 140, 141,
144, 146–7, 149–50, 152,
153, see also theology, Latin
American liberation (LALT);
theology, liberation
Llosa, Vargas 84, 86, 89
Löwy, Michael 129
Luhman, Niklas 116–7

market 15–6, 19–22, 31, 37–9,
43, 47–8, 49–50, 60, 95, see
also idolatry, market; market
system
competition 57
dynamics 1
economic rationality 56
financial 7, 77
laws 16, 18, 42, 45, 47, 50,
61–3, 71, 73, 91
logic 16, 90
priests 18
sacredness 45
transcendentalization 61–3, 95
war 37, 60
market system 3, 12, 13, 14–5,
17, 59, 70, 83, 87, 97, see also
market capacity 57
Marramao, Giacomo 56
Marxism 80, 110, 138, 142
see also Marx
Marx, Karl 2, 20, 22, 47, 55–6
see also Marxism
Mesters, Carlos 131
mimetic desire(s) 4, 35–42,
44–50, 57–60, 61
modernity 12–3, 34, 35, 40, 44,
45, 64, 137, 144, 145, 152
bourgeois 39
fundamental characteristics 43

myth of progress 12, 34, 35, 38, 41, 56, 79

need(s) 2, 31–3, 37, 39–40, 41, 42, 46, 46–7, 47, 49, 57, 60
satisfaction of basic 39, 48, 66
Nenuca 130–9, 140, 147, 149–50, 153
neoliberalism 1, 11, 15, 52, 64, 69, 72, 74, 80, 83, 87, 88, 102, 105, 121, 126
Neto, Delfin 40
Novak, Michael 19, 61, 91

Omerod, Paul 90

poor 6–8, 17–9, 23, 25, 29, 30, 31, 41, 43, 47, 49, 65, 67, 68–9, 73, 86, 91, 96, 97, 115, 125–7, 131, 133–6, 144, 147, see also poverty
dignity 24, 45
good news 26, 76
inefficiency 87
liberation 30, 105–6, 138–9, 140, 144, see also theology, liberation
life 75, 124, 142, 149
majority 53
option 53–4, 98, 100, 102, 107–8, 130, 146, 148
sacrifices 95
struggle for the life 48
Pope John Paul II 6
Popper, Karl 83, 84
poverty 30, 53, 65, 67, 69, 87, 103, 121, 122, 124, 129, see also poor
absolute 6–7
extreme 51
feminization 6
overcoming 31, 72, 104

power 1, 23, 24, 38, 39, 77, 78, 91, 106, 119–20, 139, 144, 145, 147, 149, 150, 153
desire 3
praxis 101, 102, 108, 127, 130, 131n, 149

Reich, Robert 93
reign of God 122–6, see also kingdom, God
religion(s) 1–4, 9, 10, 15, 19, 53–6, 61, 62, 76, 77, 82, 85, 90–5, 96, 98, 115n, 129, 130, 138, 142, 145
traditional 43
Robinson, Joan 11

sacrifice(s) 12, 22, 25–8, 49–50, 60, 91, 95, 96, 98, 135, 143, 144, 148, 152
human lives 62, 64, 72, 112, 115
legitimacy 18
necessary 17–9, 39, 40–5, 61, 64, 71, 90
salvation 9–10, 25, 33, 54–5, 64, 71, 90–1, 98, 123, 135, 147
Sampaio, Plinio 35
Samuelson, Paul 14, 18
Santa Ana, Julio de 115n, 144
Santos, Boaventura dos 54, 64
Segundo, Juan 64, 98
Silva, President Luiz Inácio da (Lula) 104, 105, 107
Simonsen, Mário 18
sin(s) 8, 45, 50, 72, 151
expiation 19
original 12, 15–7, 70, 120–1, 135
Smith, Adam 21, 69n, 84, 84–5
Sobrino, Jon 97
solidarity 8, 16–7, 20–1, 27, 29,

37, 49–50, 53–4, 73–4, 84,
  102–3, 105, 107, 110, 114–5,
  119, 121, 123, 146, 152–3
Soros, George 83–4, 86

temptation 8–9, 28–9, 70, 96–7,
  123, 144, 152–3
 doing good 16–7, 71
Thatcher, Margaret 81
theology 1, 3, 6, 15, 16, 19, 25,
  53–4, 55, 65, 71, 72, 91, 96,
  108–9, 112, 115, 121, 135–6,
  143, 149, 152–3, *see also*
  economic(s), theology
 endogenous 12, 94
 grace 69, 73
 implicit 12
 laissez-faire 63
 Latin American liberation
  (LALT) 4, 100–2
 liberation 1, 3, 20, 64, 98, 102,
  127–8, 129–30, 132, 136–7,
  139–40, 146–7, 148, *see also*
  poor, liberation
 prosperity 69, 73
 retribution 43, 69, 73
 sacrifice 19

sacrificial 98
Third World 34, 45, 52, 65, 90,
  101
Thurow, Lester 82–3, 89
Touraine, Alain 137

Vattimo, Gianni 150–1
Vervier, Jacques 32–3
Vigil, José 143–4
violence 44–5, 48, 58, 60–3, 67
Von Mises 84

wealth 2, 7–8, 18, 23, 26, 53,
  66, 73, 95
 accumulation 3, 14, 15, 17, 22,
  25, 31, 36, 57, 59, 70, 72
 concentration 34, 65, 78, 87
 pursuit 1, 67
 redistribution 30–3, 48
 virtual 77
Weber, Max 2, 66–7, 82
Wolfensohn, James 103
World Bank (WB) 17, 21, 42,
  78, 80, 90, 103, 117, 119
World Trade Organization
  (WTO) 21, 78, 103, 108, 117,
  119

CPSIA information can be obtained at www.ICGtesting.com
Printed in the USA
BVOW012229191212

308719BV00002B/49/P